UNDER NEW MANAGEMENT

UNDER NEW MANAGEMENT

How Leading Organizations Are
Upending Business as Usual

David Burkus

Houghton Mifflin Harcourt

BOSTON   NEW YORK

2016

For information about permission to reproduce selections from
this book, write to trade.permissions@hmhco.com or to Permissions,
Houghton Mifflin Harcourt Publishing Company, 3 Park Avenue,
19th Floor, New York, New York 10016.

www.hmhco.com

Library of Congress Cataloging-in-Publication Data
Names: Burkus, David, (date) author.
Title: Under new management : how leading organizations
are upending business as usual / David Burkus.
Description: Boston : Houghton Mifflin Harcourt, 2016.
Includes bibliographical references and index.
Identifiers: LCCN 2015037017 | ISBN 9780544630970 (hardcover)
ISBN 9780544631601 (ebook) | ISBN 9780544842151
(pbk. (international edition))
Subjects: LCSH: Management — Case studies. | Management —
Employee participation — Case studies.
Classification: LCC HD31.2 .B87 2016 | DDC 658 — dc23
LC record available at http://lccn.loc.gov/2015037017

Printed in the United States of America
DOC 10 9 8 7 6 5 4 3 2 1

To Lincoln and Harrison

Contents

Introduction:
Management Needs New Management 1

1. Outlaw Email 13
2. Put Customers Second 26
3. Lose the Standard Vacation Policy 44
4. Pay People to Quit 58
5. Make Salaries Transparent 71
6. Ban Noncompetes 86
7. Ditch Performance Appraisals 102
8. Hire as a Team 117
9. Write the Org Chart in Pencil 132
10. Close Open Offices 148
11. Take Sabbaticals 162
12. Fire the Managers 176
13. Celebrate Departures 192

Afterword:
Reinventing the Management Engine 206
Next Steps 211
Acknowledgments 212
Notes 213
Index 234
About the Author 245

UNDER NEW MANAGEMENT

Introduction:
Management Needs New Management

In 1898 the Bethlehem Iron Company was in trouble. The company was facing increased competition and losing ground quickly. Besides its misnomer company name (they actually produced steel), its share of the market as a supplier to the railroad industry was rapidly being grabbed by a growing number of Pittsburgh-based firms, including the Carnegie Steel Company.

To try to turn their fortunes around, Bethlehem Iron's leaders hired a middle-aged intellectual with an interesting past. He had studied at the renowned preparatory school Phillips Exeter Academy, with the intention of continuing his education at Harvard. But after passing the Harvard entrance exam with honors, he decided against attending. Instead, in a somewhat stunning move, he became a machinist and worked his way up the factory floor to become foreman. He studied mechanical engineering by night while he continued to work as both a laborer and a foreman by day. By 1898, having begun to merge his intellectual knowledge with his laborer's experience, he decided to become a consultant.

His name was Frederick Winslow Taylor.

Taylor brought to Bethlehem Iron a new set of tools for maximizing the efficiency of the steelworks. His method was to systematically study every task in the system of production, then eliminate unnecessary tasks and train laborers in the detailed and specific way to execute each task. After perfecting the system and the tasks, Taylor sought to perfect the laborers themselves by removing hourly wages and assigning a specific pay rate to the segment of work for which they were personally responsible.

This "piece-rate" system was seen as a way to increase the speed of production and decrease loafing among workers. Taylor himself would repeat that there was not a single manual laborer "who does not devote a considerable part of his time to studying just how slowly he can work and still convince his employer that he is going at a good pace."[1] It was Taylor's role as a consultant to study what that good pace actually was.

Taylor would also study the tools of production. In one instance, he famously asserted that the most effective load a worker should carry in a shovel was 21.5 pounds, but that workers often used the same shovel regardless of the material being loaded (and hence the weight often varied in the load they were actually carrying). Taylor found or designed new shovels for each material that would scoop exactly 21.5 pounds. Taylor viewed the discovery of such specific levels of efficiency as out of the intellectual reach of the common laborer; the ideal worker, in his mind, was simply an unskilled cog in the larger machine, trained to do just one task and rewarded when he performed that task optimally. Taylor asserted that "it is only through *enforced* standardization of methods, *enforced* adoption of the best implements and working conditions, and *enforced* cooperation that this faster work can be assured. And the duty of enforcing the adoption of standards and enforcing this cooperation rests with the *management* alone."[2] In short, Taylor didn't need the minds of laborers; he only needed their bodies.

Not surprisingly, his ideas weren't easily accepted by the laborers themselves. Taylor's rigid methods had indeed increased production, but those changes also caused strife among laborers and managers who were used to the way they had been working. By 1901 Taylor was forced to leave Bethlehem Iron after disputes with other managers. But he didn't walk away from his principles of "scientific management." Instead, he began spreading his ideas as far as he could, and he would eventually see them readily adopted.

Taylor's concept of scientific management came at exactly the right time. Just before the turn of the nineteenth century, there had rarely been a need for smart managers to supervise large groups of unskilled laborers. In 1790, 90 percent of the working population in the United States lived on farms, producing food for themselves but also items like clothing, furniture, soap, and candles.[3] What little commercial manufacturing existed was done by skilled artisans who worked in small shops that often doubled as their homes.

The industrial revolution changed all of that. As new machines were invented and ways to power those machines were discovered, the speed of production for various tasks quickened. Between 1890, just before Taylor began working with Bethlehem Iron, and 1958, manufacturing output per labor-hour in the United States grew almost fivefold (and it has kept growing rapidly ever since).[4] Products that used to be created by lone artisans were now mass-produced in large factories. Those factories needed employees. Those employees needed managers. Those managers needed tools.

Frederick Winslow Taylor provided the tools to manage the people in those factories. His ideas dramatically increased the speed and efficiency of production and helped companies grow. There are even those who say that the amazing economic growth of the twentieth century stems largely from Taylor's management ideas and the ideas they inspired. As the majority of the population moved from farm work to factory work, the style of management that fueled that growth became the unquestioned standard — the universal toolbox. Over time, others would build on Taylor's work and add more tools that built off his ideas (or sometimes were positioned as replacements for Taylor's ideas), thus becoming part of the toolbox used to manage large-scale industrial firms. Even the most drastic departures from Taylor's ideas were still tools to be used by the managers and leaders of large-scale, largely industrial firms.

Taylor's public lectures were eventually published as books. The most popular, *Principles of Scientific Management,* was published in 1911, and sales quickly took off around the country and the world, even as far as Japan.[5] (When Taylor's grandson visited Japan, he reported that managers of many companies insisted on taking their picture with him.) Taylor inspired a group of efficiency-minded managers who started a monthly magazine called *System,* which featured articles on maximizing the efficiency of all aspects of work.[6] *System* would grow in popularity and eventually take the new title of *Businessweek.*

Universities started business schools to train managers and future managers on how to use the tools of scientific management to maximize production and minimize costs. Taylor even joined one, becoming a professor at the Tuck School of Business at prestigious Dartmouth College.[7] Companies began to "benchmark" their practices by comparing their use of these tools to how the industry leaders were using them. Amazingly, many of these basic management tools are still taught at business schools and benchmarked by managers. After all, these tools got us to where we are today.

But the truth is, where we are today looks a whole lot different than where we were when Frederick Winslow Taylor first stepped onto the factory floor at Bethlehem Iron in the 1800s.

Throughout the latter part of the twentieth century, the nature of work changed dramatically for a lot of people. Instead of manual labor (performing routine tasks in the service of mass-producing a product), organizations increasingly needed their workforce to engage in *mental* labor — making decisions about redesigning products or about marketing them, or designing information technology systems, or finding new sources of capital. The volume of mental labor — or "knowledge work," as it would become known — has continued to grow. But for a very long time now, management has held on to the tools of the past — like a factory worker using the same shovel regardless of the material being shoveled.

It became obvious as early as the 1950s that the tools of "Taylorism" weren't going to work in the new world of work. William Whyte, a reporter for *Fortune* magazine, published a scathing critique in 1956 under the title *The Organization Man*.[8] In Whyte's view, the corporate structure and management tools developed under Taylor for application to factory workers was totally smothering the individual initiative and creativity of knowledge workers. Just as Taylor had done on the assembly line, management still demanded uniformity and conformity. As a result, both companies and society generally were suffering from "groupthink" — a term that Whyte coined but that Irving Janus would popularize as the tragedy of conformity destroying creativity and hindering decision-making.[9] Although readers found Whyte's observations compelling and managers sympathized with the poor souls depicted in his book, not much changed. After all, they didn't have the tools for making changes.

"As a society, we've had hundreds of years to work on managing industrial firms," says Reed Hastings, the serially disruptive founder of Netflix. "We're just beginning to learn how to run creative firms, which is quite different."[10] Hastings isn't the only leader to recognize that traditional management tools were designed for systems that rarely exist in the contemporary economy. Researchers in human behavior and organizations have long known about the gap between what science tells us about the optimal ways to lead and manage people and what best practices dictate. "We are prisoners of a traditional way of working that we inherited from the industrial era," says Julian Birkinshaw, a professor of strategy and entrepreneurship at London Business School. "We need to ask ourselves whether we can find better ways of working for the future."[11]

Fortunately, we can.

Finding a Better Way to Manage

There's no question that the ideas presented in this book will raise eyebrows. Most of them are new, radical, and even revolutionary. And you are certainly welcome to dismiss them as too outrageous to ever work.

But here's the catch. As you'll see in each chapter, these "radical" concepts are already in place in a number of well-established and forward-thinking corporations, and the truth is that not only are they working, but the organizations using them are thriving.

The purpose of this book is to challenge you and your company to ask whether the time has come for you to reexamine some of the most fundamental concepts in management today. Remember, the business of business is all about change and keeping up with the latest trends. Here's your chance to see for yourself what kinds of management changes you should be considering.

Corporate leaders, entrepreneurs, and organizational psychologists have been working to build a new set of tools — the new kind of management that managers need. They are challenging assumptions, questioning traditions, and abandoning so-called best practices. Although not every attempt at something new has worked, many new ideas are starting to show promise, and the redesigned management tools presented in this book may be among the most promising. They may seem odd, but they are effective. And decades of research in human psychology reveal why: they work because they are different *and* better. Indeed, their differentness strengthens the case that we need reinvention.

For starters, chapter 1 takes aim at one of the biggest barriers to productivity: email. Although email can make people feel more productive, corporate leaders across the globe are discovering that banning or limiting access to email makes their staffs more, not less, productive. Their experiences are matched by recent research findings that, contrary to popular belief, email actually hurts more than it helps.

Chapter 2 examines an equally radical move instigated by a global group of leaders: to best service their customers, some leaders now put their customers' needs second and their employees' needs first. They have inverted the traditional rule that the customer always comes first and aligned their practice instead with a well-researched model of achieving customer satisfaction through employee happiness.

Chapter 3 investigates the traditional vacation policy. In the industrial era, managers needed to limit employee vacations so that they would always have enough people around to run the factory. But as industrial work gave way to knowledge work, many leaders questioned whether such limits on vacation were necessary. Sounds revolutionary, to be sure, but wait and see how some new vacation policies are working out.

Chapter 4 reveals how the practice of helping employees quit (literally paying them a quitting bonus), though counterintuitive, is actually worthwhile. Companies such as Zappos and Amazon have made this practice popular. But even before Zappos and Amazon, researchers were examining phenomena like sunk costs and confirmation bias to show why quitting bonuses work, regardless of whether or not employees take the money.

Chapter 5 asks whether how much employees are paid should be public knowledge. While sharing salaries might raise privacy concerns, keeping them secret might be hurting employees even more. Research suggests that payroll secrecy lowers overall employee salaries and generates more strife and distress in the workplace than payroll transparency. After learning this lesson the hard way, leaders at companies like Whole Foods Market and SumAll opened up their payrolls for all company employees to examine.

Chapter 6 examines another area where traditional corporate secrecy often seems valuable but may actually be costly to the firm: forcing employees to sign a noncompete clause in the employment contract. New evidence from a variety of fields suggests that this long-held practice hurts not only departing employees but also those who stay with the company, and even the company itself. Read the chapter and then make up your own mind regarding the usefulness of noncompetes.

Chapter 7 argues for striking down another traditional practice that might actually be doing more harm than good. Performance appraisals have long been assumed to be of vital importance to a manager's job. But more and more companies have found that rigid performance management structures actually prevent employees from improving their performance. For example, well-known companies like Microsoft, Adobe Systems, and Motorola have all abandoned the traditional annual performance review and built more evidence-based systems that improve both employee and company performance.

Chapter 8 describes how companies are reorganizing and revolutionizing the hiring process. In most firms, managers hire by screening résumés and conducting a few interviews with individual candidates. But in practice, most managers find that a significant percentage of new employees don't perform as well as they interview. In response, many leaders have found that the best practice is to turn the hiring decision over to the entire team with whom the candidate would be working. Using the wisdom of the collective, the team members can better figure out whether the new hire will fit in with them.

Chapter 9 rethinks another widely held "best" practice — the so-called organizational chart. While constructing rigid hierarchies of employees and outlining them in a fixed structure may have worked in older industries like railroads, the ever-changing nature of work today demands an org chart that can handle those changes quickly. These days the best leaders write their organizational chart in pencil, allowing the best teams to be fluid — no matter what "divisions" they would traditionally be assigned to — and to form around problems and products. Moreover, new evidence suggests that we work best in teams that change often.

Chapter 10 reconsiders the environment in which teams work. Managers often explain the recent trend toward open offices as necessary to inspire collaboration, but the latest research and experience have shown that any benefits of open office design for collaboration are typically offset by myriad distractions. Your workplace *does* affect how you work, and the best leaders are bringing a different answer to the open versus closed office debate.

Chapter 11 investigates another different answer, this time to the question of burnout. It turns out that the best leaders find ways to give themselves and their employees long-term breaks, or sabbaticals. They have found that the best way to stay productive all of the time is to spend a good portion of time being deliberately unproductive. The findings of researchers (many of whom have themselves taken sabbaticals through their universities) back up the experience of these leaders.

Chapter 12 ponders the most intriguing modern-day management question of all: are managers even necessary? Some leaders have opted to eliminate managers altogether, while others have found ways to push some of the management function down to those who are being managed. Decades of research suggest that employees are most productive and engaged when they control their own destiny, regardless of how many managers their company has.

Chapter 13 examines a rarely considered element of managing individuals — saying good-bye. As the length of individual tenure in companies (or even industries) grows shorter all the time, leaders are saying good-bye to even their best people more frequently. How they do it, whether they celebrate or shun the departed, affects not just those leaving but those who remain.

At first blush, all of the ideas in this book will seem odd compared to business as usual, but the truth is that *business isn't usual anymore.*

Our tools may be outdated, but there is hope. Gary Hamel, one of the leading management thinkers of the past few decades, puts it this way: "If human beings could invent the modern industrial organization, then they can reinvent it."[12] The ideas being tested by both psychologists studying organizations and organizational leaders themselves might represent the reinvention that management truly needs.

These tools may look counterintuitive or strange, but then again, consider how strange Frederick Winslow Taylor's ideas must have seemed to the people inside Bethlehem Iron. Or consider how strange a large-scale factory would have looked to the craftsmen and farmers of the 1800s. The old ways of management have taken business far, but under new management, we can go even further in our changing world.

David Burkus
Fall 2015

1

■

OUTLAW EMAIL

Corporate leaders across the globe are discovering that banning or limiting their employees' access to email is making them more, not less, productive. Their experiences are matched by recent research findings that email hurts more than it helps.

W E SEND OVER 100 billion emails every day.[1] And most of them are for business purposes.

You might call that daily deluge of electronic information a symbol of technological progress, but Thierry Breton, the CEO of the France-based technology company Atos SE, sees it differently. He likens that volume of emails to pollution — email pollution. When Breton realized that the constant stream of emails was distracting to both him and the people in his company, he took steps to eliminate what he believed were negative effects on company productivity.

In February 2011, Breton announced that he was banning email. In three years' time, he wanted Atos to be an "email-zero" company. "We are producing data on a massive scale that is fast polluting our working environments and also encroaching into our personal lives," Breton said in a public statement released through Atos's website. "We are taking action now to reverse this trend, just as organizations took measures to reduce environmental pollution after the industrial revolution."[2]

That statement is surprising for a variety of reasons. For one, Atos isn't exactly anti-technology: the company is a leading information technology services firm. Atos isn't a small start-up either: at the time of the announcement, the company employed over 70,000 people in more than forty offices around the world. But Atos's massive size was actually what Breton saw as the reason for the communication clog. "The volume of emails we send and receive is unsustainable for business," he said. "Managers spend between 5 and 20 hours a week reading and writing emails." Breton, likewise, isn't exactly the model of a rogue start-up founder testing out wild new ways to work. Instead, he's a middle-aged former minister of finance for France and a former professor at Harvard Business School. Needless to say, he'd put a lot of thought behind his assertion that "email is on the way out as the best way to run a company and do business."

Breton actually adopted the zero-email philosophy for himself long before he announced it to the company. He'd stopped using internal email nearly five years earlier, when he was working for the French government, because he found it wasn't helping him get his work done well.[3] Breton found something similar with the staff of Atos, even if they couldn't see the solution right away. Atos polled a sample of 300 employees and monitored the volume of their email. In just one week, the 300 employees sent or received over 85,000 messages.[4] When the company surveyed employees, it found that the majority of them felt that they couldn't keep up with their emails, that the time spent trying was time wasted, and that the effort to stay current with email kept them from dealing with more important tasks. Breton found that his employees were realizing the same thing he'd discovered years before. So he simply banned email.

Of course, Atos didn't ban communication, and it didn't even ban electronic communication. Instead, Atos tried to find a better tool for managing internal communication. The company bought another software firm called BlueKiwi and used its technology to build its own social network for the entire enterprise. The network was organized around 7,500 open communities that employees can join. These communities represent products, internal programs, and myriad other projects needing collaboration. Unlike email, these communities are totally transparent, so newcomers can see all of the communication about particular issues. Like email, conversations are threaded so that newcomers to the community can see the past history of the discussion. Unlike email, however, conversations are not digitally pushed to employees' inboxes, interrupting their focused work time. Instead, employees can choose to enter the discussion on their terms.

The social network also makes it easier for employees to find needed experts, share knowledge companywide, and, most importantly, collaborate better. And the new system has dramatically cut down on internal email. To help its managers adjust, Atos even created training programs for more than 5,000 managers to teach them how to lead their departments and projects in a zero-email environment. The company also trained 3,500 "ambassadors" to provide training and support among their peers as they adjusted to the new system. Now fully converted to the new system, the company certifies projects and communication processes as "zero-email."

The initiative appears to be working. Although Atos didn't hit its target, a study conducted in 2014 by an independent firm showed that Atos's email reduction efforts were progressing very nicely. By the end of 2013, Atos had certified 220 programs as "zero-email" and reduced overall email 60 percent, going from an average of 100 email messages per week per employee to less than 40.

More importantly, employees now report feeling far more productive and collaborative. Collaboration has been enhanced by the internal social network, which doesn't distract employees by pinging messages to their inbox and actually provides a better-designed platform for group communication. Atos employees post in the company's internal communities almost 300,000 times a month, and those messages are viewed nearly 2 million times per month. Most importantly, all of those views are by choice.

These email reduction efforts have been good for the company as well: Atos's operating margin increased from 6.5 percent to 7.5 percent in 2013, earnings per share rose by more than 50 percent, and administrative costs declined from 13 percent to 10 percent. Obviously, not all of these improvements were the result of banning email, but the correlation is certainly strong. So is the empirical evidence.

The Revolution Against Email

Thierry Breton isn't the only technology leader openly criticizing email. Phil Libin, the CEO and founder of Evernote, feels that the problem with email is not just volume but also how that volume is dealt with. "A concept like an email inbox is harmful. It's bad for you. It's bad for productivity. Think about what your inbox is. Your email inbox is a list of things that you're behind on, sorted in the wrong order. It's not how you want to work," Libin said.[5] "Email is fine if you're maybe getting two or three a day. It was never meant for anything like the volume we currently see."

Jay Simons, the president of Australia-based software firm Atlassian, also thinks that the reason email is so damaging is that it's used wrongly and too often.[6] "We use it for so many things that it's not really appropriate for. Email is really good at being a directive communications notifier," he said. "If you're expecting any meaningful discussion, email is probably not a great forum."

Thierry Breton and Atos aren't even the only ones to ban email. Cristian Rennella, cofounder of the South American travel comparison website el Mejor Trato (eMT), found that his team was really good at responding to email, but that email was also really good at distracting his team. So he banned it, or at least banned all internal emails. Employees resisted at first, but after a three-month trial period everyone was on board. "There's no way we are going back to email," Rennella said.[7] "We have efficiency." Rennella's firm is a much smaller company than Atos, but the logistics of banning email may have been even harder to implement, since the company has no office and all employees work virtually. Like Atos, eMT built an internal communication network that it uses to manage projects and communication. Also like the Atos system, eMT's system features no notifications or alerts that interrupt a focused employee.

A number of different studies conducted recently support these leaders' assertions that email isn't the best tool for staying productive and stress-free. Many surveys show that the experience of Atos employees mirrors the average employee's. In 2014 over 108 billion email messages were sent and received every day.[8] Email occupies 23 percent of the average employee's workday, and that average employee checks his or her email 36 times an hour.[9]

One research study even supports Breton's moratorium on internal email. Researchers Gloria Mark and Stephen Voida from the University of California at Irvine and Armand Cardello from the US Army cut off email usage for thirteen civilian information workers and measured the effects of the cutoff in a variety of ways.[10] The researchers first took participants through a three-day baseline period in which they were interviewed and observed visually and using computer monitoring software. Mark and her colleagues even measured the participants' heart rates (as a proxy for stress levels). Then they pulled the plug on email. Specifically, they installed a filter on participants' email program that would file away all incoming messages for later reading and remove all notifications of the incoming messages. (Participants were allowed to access the emails they received prior to the cutoff day.)

This "no-email" condition continued for five days, during which time the researchers continued to observe the participants, track their computer usage, and measure their heart rates. With no access to email, participants changed their habits: they began to communicate face-to-face and over the telephone more frequently. The researchers also noticed that all except one participant spent significantly more time in each computer program; this observation suggests that participants were more focused on the tasks in front of them and less distracted by attempts to multitask email communication alongside their intended work project. They also experienced significantly less stress during the no-email period than measured during the baseline. In short, *participants were more focused and less stressed when they couldn't use email.* Participants noticed this effect as well. They consistently reported feeling more relaxed and focused, as well as more productive, with their email shut off than under normal working conditions.

The productivity finding is particularly interesting: we often feel more productive once we've cleaned out our email inbox, despite perhaps not accomplishing anything value-creating for our organization. These researchers' findings certainly suggest that Breton's zero-email policy had a positive effect on his company's productivity and profitability.

Gloria Mark believes that making no-email a company policy may have been what made it so effective. "It's really an organizational mandate, because if any single individual tries to pull out of this email web, they're going to be penalized and out of the loop," she said.[11]

Without knowing about Mark's research, Shayne Hughes recreated the experiment on his own employees. Hughes serves as the president of Learning as Leadership, a California-based organizational development consulting firm, and in 2012 he issued an executive order forbidding internal email communication for one week.[12]

Hughes's employees were skeptical at first, wondering how they would accomplish anything without email as a collaboration tool. Some employees thought the company would be in chaos or grind to a halt. But as the week progressed the team found that email had actually been a pretty blunt tool. Old-school methods like face-to-face conversations and the telephone were much more useful. "Outlawing internal email for a week challenged us not only to be more thoughtful about what we worked on but also to be more deliberate about what we address and with whom," Hughes recalled.[13]

Hughes also found that during the week he outlawed email the whole company's stress level decreased and their productivity level increased. "When we stopped sending one another e-mail, we stopped winding one another up," Hughes recalled. "The decrease in stress from one day to the next was palpable. So was our increase in productivity"—just as Mark's research would have predicted. "Whether it was the trust built when two team members worked through a conflict or the unexpected creativity we accessed when we tackled a problem together, communicating reconnected us with the neglected power of human interaction."

Putting Limits on Email

While Gloria Mark's research certainly lends support to Atos's zero-email policy and Shayne Hughes's week off from email, Mark herself prefers less drastic measures. "I think that people should restrict reading emails to limited times during the day instead of continually checking it," she said.[14] Rather than going without email entirely, using it in moderation seems more reasonable to her. Interestingly, other research suggests that limiting email checks to certain times is just as effective as banning it completely. A policy of moderation in email use might be enough to bring about the same decreases in stress and increases in productivity.

Researchers from the University of British Columbia designed a two-week-long experiment in which individuals toggled between checking email at will and restricting the number of times they checked it.[15] The researchers randomly assigned volunteers to one of two groups. The first group was instructed to check their email as often as they could (the aptly named "unlimited-email" condition); the second group was instructed to limit their email checking to only three times per day and to keep their email program closed the rest of the day (the equally aptly named "limited-email" condition).

One week into the experiment, the groups' instructions were switched so that the first group took on the limited-email condition and the second group the unlimited-email condition. At 5:00 p.m. every weekday of the study (presumably the end of the workday), all participants were sent a link to complete a survey with a variety of measurements that were designed to evaluate their level of distraction, stress, positive or negative emotions, well-being, feelings of connectedness, quality of sleep, and even feelings of meaningfulness in life. Similar to the no-email study, these researchers' findings showed that participants reported significantly less stress when they were working under the limited-email condition than under the unlimited-email condition.

When in the limited-email condition, participants also felt much less distracted and better able to focus. Although stress itself was the only direct effect linked to the reduction in email, the reports of lowered stress were also associated with other positive results, such as social connection, sleep quality, and even finding meaning in life. Interestingly, the effect of limiting email on lowering stress was found to be about as strong as the effects of many common relaxation techniques, such as slow breathing and peaceful imagination. In other words, limiting email may not bring people to their happy place, *but it will lower stress just as much as being there.*

Researchers believe that limiting email decreases stress and increases productivity because it cuts back on multitasking and distraction. "Email increases multitasking," said Kostadin Kushlev, the lead author on the limited-email study. "It fragments our attention and contributes to our feeling that there is too much to do and not enough time to do it."[16] A significant body of work suggests that when two tasks require the same level of cognitive resources (working memory), people cannot perform them simultaneously. Because of the amount of focus and thought required, they don't actually multitask but instead switch between the two tasks, juggling them back and forth. This explains why many of us can drive normally while listening passively to the radio, but using a smartphone to talk, text, or compose email harms our driving ability almost as much as driving while intoxicated.[17]

Beyond dealing with the cognitive load on working memory of executing two tasks at the same time, the switching back and forth makes further demands on working memory. To make matters worse, some theories suggest that approaching the limits of our working memory leaves us even more prone to distraction — and hence likely to toss one more weight onto our cognitive load. With notifications received every time a new email arrives, email inboxes are perfectly designed to encourage task-switching. Moreover, the inbox is often designed so that users see both the current email and a list of several other emails awaiting attention. Even worse, most of us leave our email program running in the background, drawing us away from whatever other computer programs we are working in and luring our attention back to the inbox. By leading us to task-switch, email not only increases our stress but actually reduces the quality of our overall work. That explains why participants in both studies who limited or eliminated email in their workday reported feeling more productive. "Multitasking often feels exciting, and we may feel like we are getting a lot done," said Kushlev. "But this subjective feeling is an illusion."[18]

Beyond reducing our ability to focus on the present job, work email can also encroach on our ability to focus at home, unsettling whatever work-life balance we're seeking. So while only a few companies have taken the leap that Thierry Breton called for at Atos, many companies have taken steps to limit email to normal workday hours.

In 2011, a few months after Atos's zero-email policy went into effect, the automaker Volkswagen agreed to cease email communication outside of normal business hours.[19] The company configured its email servers to stop sending or receiving email from German staff members thirty minutes after the end of the workday and to resume the connection thirty minutes before the next workday begins. Volkswagen staff can still use the phones to make calls and to browse the Internet after hours, but no new emails come through and any emails that they compose aren't sent until the server connection is turned back on. The limited-email policy applies only to staff working under trade union–negotiated contracts and not to senior management. Shortly after Volkswagen adopted the policy, the German Labor Ministry adopted it for its own staff and recommended that other companies follow suit and, at the very least, establish clear guides for staff email usage.[20] Even today as some of Volkswagen's other practices are being called deceitful, the practice of limiting email is catching on in a positive way.

Later, after this announcement in Germany, news came from France that an agreement had been signed between prominent French labor unions and employers in the technology and consulting industries. The agreement covered about 250,000 "autonomous employees" and specified an obligation to disconnect communication tools so that employees would not be interrupted during their time off from the office. The employees affected were exempt from France's standard thirty-five-hour workweek and hence worked weekends and sometimes thirteen-hour days. The agreement specified that these employees had to have at least one day off every seven days, with no email communication during their time off.[21]

Perhaps the most novel anti-email tactic was put into place by the German automaker Daimler. The Volkswagen rival took aim, not at after-hours email, but at vacation email. In 2014 the company installed a new program on its email servers that lets employees select a "Mail on Holiday" out-of-office reply.[22] Like traditional out-of-office programs, when an employee receives an email, the sender automatically receives a message that the employee is out of the office and will return on a specified date. Unlike traditional programs, however, *the program then notifies the sender that the email will be deleted and requests that the sender either resend it on the employee's return date or send it to a specified alternative person who is not away from the office.* Vacationing employees are spared from seeing (and thinking about) emails during their time off, and often they return to an empty email inbox as well. The program is optional, but available to about 100,000 employees throughout Germany.

Although an after-hours email ban can seem to be just a work-life balance initiative, research suggests that such bans can serve the greater purpose of keeping employees engaged and satisfied with their jobs. Recent research conducted by Marcus Butts, William Becker, and Wendy Boswell shows that people who receive email after work get angry more often than not and that their anger interferes with their personal lives.[23]

Every day for seven days, the researchers surveyed 341 working adults on their feelings about receiving after-work email. Each day participants received an email sometime between 5:00 p.m. and 6:00 p.m. with a link to that day's survey. Participants were instructed to complete the survey while thinking about the email they had received most recently after work hours, and to not complete the survey if they had received no emails after work that day. Participants were surveyed on a variety of items, from their perception of the tone of voice in the email, the time required to respond, the emotions they felt, and whether or not the email affected their nonwork life. They were also surveyed at the very beginning of the study on issues such as their perception of supervisor abuse and their preferences for blending their work and nonwork lives.

When they analyzed the collected data, Marcus Butts and his colleagues found that when employees received an email after work that they perceived as negative in tone, it was more likely to make them angry, decrease their happiness, and affect their nonwork life. When employees received emails they perceived as positive in tone, they were more likely to be happy, but that happiness was only fleeting. Regardless of tone, if responding to the email required a lot of time, it was likely to make employees upset. "The after-hours emails really affected those workers' personal lives," said Butts.[24] In addition to showing that after-hours emails interfere with employees' personal lives, the researchers also found a relationship between employees' perceptions that their supervisor was abusive or micromanaging and the likelihood that reading the email would make them angry.

In short, after-hours email can interfere not only with nonwork relationships but also with work relationships, specifically by increasing any preexisting tension between employees and their bosses. The researchers suggest that managers take these findings seriously and compose after-hours emails with caution, and also that employees who are angered by after-hours emails consider leaving and moving to a company with an email limitation policy (like Atos, el Mejor Trato, Learning as Leadership, or Daimler).

Whether or not company leadership decides to restrict email, limit how often employees check it, or ban it entirely, both the research and the recent experiences of these companies make a strong case that email is not the most effective tool for communication. Beyond interfering with your work-life balance, it can also have a detrimental impact on your productivity. Clearing out your email inbox can make you feel really good — like you're ultra-productive. But unless your job is to delete emails, time spent in your inbox may not be time spent wisely.

2

■

PUT CUSTOMERS SECOND

To better serve their customers, some corporate leaders have found that they must put their customers' needs second and their employees' needs first. They have basically inverted the hierarchy and aligned their companies with a well-researched model of customer satisfaction that comes through employee happiness.

IN FEBRUARY 2006, Vineet Nayar, the president and CEO of HCL Technologies, made a shocking announcement to a global meeting of HCLT's biggest customers.[1] In short, he told his customers that HCLT had decided that taking care of them was no longer his top priority. In fact, HCLT had decided to fire some of its customers.

Specifically, Nayar was announcing a reorganization of HCLT's structure and its priorities around a new strategy that he labeled "employees first, customers second." The announcement must have come as a shock to the assembly of 300 customer representatives, most of whom were from the senior leadership of their companies. However, Nayar's decision was the end result of a long period of thought and reflection by Nayar and his own senior leadership. HCLT needed to change to stay competitive, and Nayar's bold plan was to focus less on competing for customers in the short term and more on serving employees in order to win in the long term.

Nayar had taken the CEO seat after a long time with HCL Technologies. He started with the company in 1985, when it was still a small start-up with $10 million in sales. Eventually, he founded a smaller, entrepreneurial venture called Comnet inside of the HCLT parent company, and Comnet would grow quickly, along with the rest of HCLT. In 2000 HCLT had grown to one of the largest IT service providers in India, with $5 billion in revenue, and much of that revenue came from HCL Technologies.

From 2000 to 2005, however, the company started losing ground to its competitors. Although, as a company, HCLT was still growing 30 percent a year, its competitors were growing even faster, at 40 to 50 percent, and HCLT was falling to the bottom of the rankings. In 2005, when Nayar was moved to the helm of HCLT, the company was stuck in the middle of the pack and facing lots of problems, including low morale and a turnover rate of 17 percent — far higher than its competitors.

The impetus for Nayar's transformation came from two separate but similar customer interactions he had. In both, Nayar met with a customer and with several HCLT employees to debrief. The first meeting was with the CIO of a global company for which HCLT had just successfully completed a significant and time-critical project. Nayar entered the conference room to find that the CIO and HCLT employees were already assembled.

To his surprise, the CIO nearly ignored Nayar's entrance. "I was expecting to get a big smile and a handshake from him, to accept a pat on the back, and to hear champagne corks popping," Nayar recalled. Instead, the CIO focused his attention on Nayar's employees. He praised their hard work, the quality of their service, and how enjoyable it was to work with them as a team. Then he briefly turned to Nayar to say how lucky Nayar was to have these employees on board at HCLT. "I was surprised and touched by the emotion in his voice."[2]

In the second meeting, Nayar was again assembled with HCLT employees and another of their corporate customers, but this time to debrief on a failed project. Nayar expected to apologize, explain the reasons for the failures, and then outline a plan to correct their mistakes. But before he could apologize, the customer spoke up, looking Nayar directly in the eyes. "Vineet, your people did everything they could. The problem was that your organization didn't support them properly. If it had, I'm sure they would have been able to meet our objectives."[3] Nayar was surprised by how angry the customer was with him and HCLT, but struck by the fact that he held no animosity toward the team he'd been working with.

These two memorable interactions, and a host of others with customers and employees, led Nayar to rethink how HCLT was creating and capturing value. Nayar started reflecting on what he called the "value zone," the place where value was created for customers. If HCLT was truly a service-based business, serving the IT needs of its customers, then the value zone needed to be on the front lines, where employees interacted directly with customers. Those employees played the most important role in bringing real value to customers, and the rest of HCLT, he realized, should be thought of as "enabling functions."

HCLT, like a lot of organizations, had shifted its focus as it had grown. As the company grew from $10 million to $5 billion, layers and hierarchy had to be constructed to manage the larger company. Support functions had to be added to help frontline employees do their best work. As often happens, however, eventually power shifted from the frontline employees to the hierarchy and the support functions. Since managers had the power, frontline roles were being held responsible to the management positions that had been designed to aid them. Information flowed down, and accountability flowed up. If HCLT was going to refocus itself on the value zone, then it needed to reverse this flow. It needed to turn its hierarchy upside down.

Turning the hierarchy upside down required making managers accountable to frontline employees and ensuring that those in the support functions (finance, training, human resources, and so on) actually supported the frontline employees, instead of insisting that they follow the hierarchy's rigid systems. Turning around a 55,000-person organization and inverting it to put the 100 senior managers at the bottom is no small feat. Nayar focused his attention on two areas to ensure that the management and support functions served the front line: reversing accountability and building transparency.

Nayar sought to reverse accountability by making sure that the hierarchy was responsible to the front line, not the other way around. Nayar wanted the entire chain of command, up to himself as the CEO, to be *supporting* the frontline employees — not *commanding* and *controlling* them. This tactic for reversing accountability was borrowed directly from HCLT's existing customer service system. Called the "smart service desk," it worked by creating tickets for customer issues and using them to track progress as the issues worked their way through HCLT to resolution.

HCLT created a similar system for frontline employees. Whenever employees had a problem or just needed more information, they could open a support ticket that would be sent to the relevant department or support function for handling. A support ticket might need to travel through multiple departments, but that movement was tracked through the system. Most importantly, only the employee who created the ticket had the authority to close it. HCLT even changed the performance metrics for its support functions to include how many tickets were opened, how many were closed, and how long it took to resolve issues. Beyond just ensuring that frontline employees had the resources they needed, the support ticket system sent a clear and direct message to both the front line and the support roles about who was accountable to whom.

In building transparency, Nayar was targeting the veil between frontline employees and managers. Managers had access to information about the front line, but that information didn't flow in the opposite direction. To make information more transparent, Nayar created an open 360-degree feedback system. Like a lot of companies, HCLT was already using a 360-degree feedback process, but also as in a lot of companies, that process was limited in scope and only managers could influence those limits. Managers were evaluated by a small group of people within their own sphere of influence — direct reports, peer managers, and their superiors. "In other words," Nayar explains, "the review was conducted by members of a kind of good old boys' club. Because they all had to review each other, they would scratch each other's back, give each other high marks, say only nice things, and ignore problems."[4]

Nayar changed this process by allowing anyone who'd had a significant interaction with a manager to be a part of the evaluation. "Any employee could choose to do a 360-degree evaluation of any of the managers they believed had an influence — positive or negative — on their ability to do their job." Moreover, the results of those evaluations were also open. "We decided to allow anyone who had given feedback to a manager to see the results of that manager's 360."

This change took some time to be accepted by HCLT's 2,000+

managers, all of whom were given the initial choice to open their feedback for viewing. In the first year, only Nayar and a few other corporate officers made their feedback public, but eventually the majority of managers followed suit. "If they didn't, it suggested they had something to hide."[5] By making their feedback public, managers were publicly declaring their acceptance of the feedback and committing to change — all in the service of better supporting frontline employees.

In addition to making feedback transparent, Nayar also sought to bring strategic discussions out of the boardroom and to involve all employees. This began as a series of informal discussions with employees and developed into a regular series called "Directions." Prior to these events, Nayar and the senior leadership team created a video outlining the company's strategy. Then the team hit the road and traveled for two weeks of meetings with employees. The goal of Directions was to ensure that all employees were fully informed on the company's objectives and how their work contributed to those objectives. In addition, Directions ensured that all employees were speaking the same language and were given a chance to have any of their questions answered personally. To keep the conversation going, Nayar also created an online forum where employees could post any question they wanted and receive a personal response from Nayar himself.

It took time and a lot of focus on reversing accountability and building transparency, but eventually things began to turn around. Eventually, HCLT had not only inverted its hierarchy but completely reversed its situation. By 2009, the company was ranked as the best employer in India. And that recognition came with some great benefits: HCLT's annual revenue almost tripled and its market capitalization doubled. In 2013, Nayar retired from the lead role at HCLT, but the concept of employees first, customers second, remains at the core of the company's management philosophy. And it continues to fuel HCLT's success. In 2014 the company saw revenues of nearly $5.7 billion.[6]

Profiting from Putting
Your Customers Second

Nayar's idea of putting employees before customers was a novel idea for his company and his industry, but in truth, it wasn't an entirely new idea. Over twenty years earlier, a group of business professors from Harvard University had been working on a model that would have predicted exactly the outcome Nayar experienced. James Heskett, Thomas Jones, Gary Loveman, W. Earl Sasser, and Leonard Schlesinger were comparing results from their own studies and synthesizing other research to construct a model to explain the outstanding success of the most profitable service-based companies.[7]

It began with Sasser's research, conducted with his former student Fred Reichheld.[8] The duo took aim at a long-standing assumption of business — that market share is the primary driver of profitability. If a company can increase market share, the thinking went, it will increase sales while taking advantage of economies of scale to lower costs and thus increase profits. When the pair examined a variety of companies and the existing research, however, they found that market share is one factor in profitability but that another factor better explains the most profitable companies: customer loyalty. Based on their research, Sasser and Reichheld estimated that a mere 5 percent increase in customer loyalty can yield a 25 to 85 percent increase in profitability. This finding laid the foundation for the five Harvard professors' search for the causes of customer loyalty. After studying dozens of companies and troves of research, they created a model that tracked the origins of customer loyalty. They called it the "service-profit chain."

The service-profit chain links together several elements of the business model in a linear relationship: Profit and growth are driven by customer loyalty. Loyalty is influenced by customer satisfaction. Customer satisfaction is stimulated by a high perception of value of the service. Value is the result of productive employees. Productivity stems from employee satisfaction.

Simply put, *profits are driven by customer loyalty, customer loyalty is driven by employee satisfaction, and employee satisfaction is driven by putting employees first.*

Employee satisfaction is created when companies focus on creating high "internal service quality"— the term the Harvard professors used to explain job design, organizational development, training, rewards, and everything else that Nayar would have called "putting employees first." At the core of their service-profit chain was the concept of value. In a service business model, value is as much about perception of the service received as the quality of the product. Therefore, the professors theorized, satisfied and productive employees are better able to ensure that interactions with customers are high-quality and lead to a higher perception of value. The service-profit chain predicts that by putting employees first, customers will be better served and become more loyal and the company will become more profitable—exactly what Nayar and HCLT experienced.

When their research was first published, the concept of the service-profit chain generated a lot of discussion. It was a theoretical model built on a variety of research, and it led to a wave of even more research seeking to strengthen the link between satisfied employees and satisfied, profitable customers. In a recent study, Steven Brown and Son Lam of the University of Houston synthesized decades of research to firmly establish that link.[9]

Brown and Lam gathered twenty-eight studies on employee satisfaction and customers' perceptions of quality. In total, these studies examined over 6,600 employees and customers. Brown and Lam's results showed that, across all of the studies, high levels of customer satisfaction and perceived service quality were related to high levels of employee satisfaction. Frontline employees provide better service to customers when they're supported and satisfied in their work.

Most interestingly, since Brown and Lam were synthesizing a variety of studies from many different industries, they were able to analyze the employee-customer relationship in two different types of businesses: those in which customers and employees have an ongoing relationship (such as doctor's offices or IT consulting firms) and those in which the interaction takes place in a onetime transaction, such as in a fast-food restaurant or a retail shop. They assumed that, since ongoing relationships include more frequent customer-employee interactions, the effect of employee satisfaction on customers' perceptions of quality and satisfaction would be stronger in that type of business. However, they found that this effect did not change significantly with the type of business or the level of interaction with the customer. Employee satisfaction appears to have just as strong an effect on customers whether the employees interact with customers only once or their interactions are frequent and ongoing. These results echo what HCLT experienced when it put employees first and trusted them to take care of HCLT's customers.

New research also supports Nayar's ideas about flipping the organization chart. A recent study demonstrated that managers play a significant role in employees' satisfaction and the service-profit chain.[10] A trio of researchers led by Richard Netemeyer of the University of Virginia collected data from a single retail chain that included 306 store managers, 1,615 customer-employee interactions, and 57,656 customers. The researchers were testing the effect of managers' performance and satisfaction on employees, and hence its effect on customers' satisfaction and the overall performance of the managers' stores.

They found that managers' actions, customer satisfaction, and store financial performance were indeed linked. These results support the argument that management's support of employees significantly contributes to what Heskett and his colleagues at Harvard call internal service quality, the first link in the service-profit chain. The findings from the research of Netemeyer and his team also suggest that flipping the organizational chart, as Nayar did at HCLT, really works. It's essential that managers understand that their role is to support employee satisfaction and hence customer satisfaction, in no small part because their success in this role clearly has a major impact on the financial performance of their company.

The Many Ways to Put Employees First

Just as the research suggests, the significant effect of employee satisfaction on customer satisfaction can be seen not only in service industries, where employees and customers develop long-term relationships, but also in areas where the interactions are infrequent or even onetime, such as retail. Putting customers second is how the Wegman family created and grew one of the most respected grocery chains in the United States, Wegmans Food Markets. Wegmans is a family-owned business of more than eighty supermarkets with a dedicated customer base but an even more dedicated group of employees.

Founded in 1916 by John and Walter Wegman, the company is now run by Walter's grandson, Danny Wegman, whose two daughters also work in the company. With each generation, the Wegman family passes along its firm dedication to its employees and its trust in those employees to be equally dedicated to customers.[11]

Wegmans shows its commitment to employees in a variety of ways. Most overtly, the company has a long-standing no-layoff policy. In its recruiting, the company's primary requirement for hiring is a strong interest in food, and candidates who lack a passion for learning more about food are rejected. Once Wegmans finds passionate people, it invests significant time and money in training them. New employees in customer-facing positions go through up to fifty-five hours of initial training before hitting the floor.[12]

Cashiers, for example, are not allowed to talk to customers until they have completed forty hours of primary training.[13] For ongoing training, the company even sends individuals overseas on training trips.[14] Cheese department employees may be sent to Italy to learn about how Parmesan is made, and bakery employees may be sent to France to learn the French style of baking. Wegmans invests all this training in employees so that they will bring their expertise to customer interactions, advising customers on everything from foods to pair together to how best to cook and serve a meal. In addition to knowledge, Wegmans also gives its employees power. Every employee is trusted and empowered to do whatever is required to ensure that customers leave the store happy.

Just as the company puts its trust in employees, it lets them know that they can trust the company. Wegmans offers health and life insurance to all full-time employees after ninety days, and to part-timers after one year. Initially, the company paid 100 percent of the cost of these benefits. As those costs rose, managers and those making over a certain amount (in a move symbolic of Wegmans's priorities) were the first to be required to contribute to these costs. Eventually, with costs continuing to rise, every employee was required to pay a small part of the premiums.

In addition, Wegmans offers extensive education benefits. Full-time and part-time employees are eligible for tuition reimbursement and scholarships so long as they work a certain number of hours and maintain good grades. Every year the company pays over $4 million in education expenses for its employees, and employees don't take the money and run. They stay at Wegmans. Many of the long-tenured employees in the company began on the front lines. Annual turnover is typically half of what other supermarkets face.[15]

Moreover, Wegmans has been ranked highly on *Fortune*'s "Best Companies to Work For" list every year since it was started, and in 2005 it was ranked number one. Because it is a great place to work, its workers make it a great place to shop. The company's sales per square foot are often 50 percent higher than competitors' sales.[16] In addition, the home office receives thousands of emails and letters every year from customers begging them to open a new store closer to their neighborhood so that they could shop at Wegmans even more. The company, however, is committed to growing at a slower pace than customers would like. It usually opens only two or three stores a year, a pace that the company believes will allow proper investment in new employees and ensure that the Wegmans culture is not diluted.

Wegmans isn't the only example of a company with infrequent customer interactions that still benefits from putting employees first. Danny Meyer, a restaurateur and founder of Union Square Hospitality Group, has been putting employees in front of his guests for over thirty years. What Meyer calls "the virtuous cycle of enlightened hospitality" looks an awful lot like the service-profit chain. "When I first walk into any restaurant or any business, I can immediately guess what type of experience I'm in for by sensing whether the staff members appear to be focused on their work, supportive of one another, and enjoying one another's company," he says.[17]

Meyer's virtuous cycle strategy has worked everywhere from his original Union Square Café to the global burger chain Shake Shack. Meyer believes that in order to satisfy his customers, he needs to put them second. "The interests of our own employees must be placed directly ahead of those of our guests because the only way we can consistently earn raves, win repeat business, and develop bonds of loyalty with our guests is to first ensure that our own team members feel jazzed about coming to work." Meyer also believes that in order to please his investors, he needs to put them last. "But not because I don't want to earn a lot of money," he says. "On the contrary, I staunchly believe that standing conventional business priorities on their head ultimately leads to even greater, more enduring financial success."[18]

Meyer and Union Square put employees first in a variety of ways. Besides making sure that their financial needs are met through great wages and benefits, the company also seeks out employees' feedback and lets them know that they are heard on everything from assessing individual managers to providing feedback at their own restaurant or another restaurant in the company. The company has often taken action on, or even fired, a manager who was found not to be inspiring the hospitality standards of the company. Meyer also gives some managers the opportunity to become owners by allowing them to earn or purchase a stake in the restaurant they manage. In 2015, just before he took the burger chain Shake Shack public, all managers at every location were granted stock options.[19] In addition, regular full-time and even part-time employees were given a chance to buy stock at the pre-IPO list price of $21 — which paid off significantly the next day when the stock closed 150 percent higher at $45.90.

Wegmans and Union Square Hospitality Group are testaments that everybody wins when leaders build a culture that puts frontline employees first and managers are accountable to them as they serve employees. When managers focus their attention elsewhere and the culture becomes flat, frontline employees divert their attention away from customers, and customers then eventually give their attention to another company.

It is especially easy for a company to make this mistake when it is successful and growing quickly. That's the lesson Howard Schultz and Starbucks learned around 2007, when the store had grown too quickly and in-store performance began to suffer. Schultz had been a key figure at Starbucks almost from its beginning. Though not technically a founder, Schultz was responsible for creating the much-loved coffee chain, and he has also been responsible for bringing it back from the brink by focusing less on its growth plan and more on its "partners" (the Starbucks term for employees).

Born in 1953, Schultz grew up in a housing project in Brooklyn.[20] His early childhood experiences would have a dramatic effect on his strong belief in putting employees first. Schultz's father held a variety of blue-collar jobs, none of which included benefits like health insurance. At age seven, Schultz witnessed his family suffering immensely after his father broke his ankle and lost his job as a delivery truck driver. The family struggled to keep food on the table while his father healed, and Shultz never forgot that difficult time. It would later have a significant impact on his leadership.

After finishing college on an athletic scholarship, Schultz became a salesman at Xerox and excelled so quickly that, at just twenty-six years old, he was headhunted to become the vice president and general manager of Hammarplast, an American subsidiary of the Swedish housewares maker Perstorp AB. One of Hammarplast's products was an espresso machine, and one of its best customers was a coffee roaster in Seattle named Starbucks.

After flying out to visit Starbucks, Schultz decided to move to Seattle and join the coffee company as part owner and head of marketing. He stayed only four years: after a trip to Italy convinced him that Starbucks should bring the Italian espresso bar model to the United States but he couldn't convince his partners, he decided to launch his own company. When Schultz learned a few years later that his former partners were looking to sell Starbucks, he acquired the company and merged it with his own venture.

As the leader of Starbucks, Schultz believed that the best way to scale was to improve customer experience — and that the best way to do that was to engage the frontline employees. "We believed the best way to meet and exceed the expectations of our customers was to hire and train great people," Schultz said. "We invested in employees who were zealous about good coffee."[21] Schultz created extensive training programs designed to invest in and develop partners who would thrive working behind a counter and interacting with customers.

Partly influenced by his childhood and partly to underscore the importance of the frontline partners, Schultz began offering comprehensive health care coverage for all partners, even part-time workers who logged more than twenty hours per week. Under Schultz's leadership and with the company's investment in its partners, Starbucks bloomed. In 2000, Schultz stepped down as CEO (but remained chairman of the board). The company had grown dramatically, opening over 1,000 stores in his last year alone.[22] Without Schultz's emphasis on the partners, however, that growth rate would end up becoming a problem.

A few years later, in 2007, Schultz grew concerned about Starbucks's pace of growth. Schultz had observed a dilution of the

"Starbucks experience," triggered by a lot of missing, or watered-down, elements. Customer interactions seemed to lack a human connection. For example, few baristas seemed to remember regular customers' names. Store managers didn't seem proud of their work or invested in their store. Many were focused too much on making numbers and not enough on modeling the company's values. "We have an enormous responsibility to both the people who have come before us and to the 150,000 partners and their families who are relying on our stewardship," Schultz wrote in a memo to senior leaders.

A few days after he sent the memo, it was leaked to the press and a wave of discussion about the Starbucks brand and the company's feasibility ensued. Later in 2007, Starbucks's financials started to echo Schultz's concerns. Although its year-over-year revenues were positive, the percentage of increase was smaller than the company's average. In 2008, Starbucks announced that Schultz would be returning to the role of CEO.

To turn Starbucks around, Schultz knew what his priorities were. "Perhaps the most important step in improving the faltering US business was to reengage our partners, especially those on the front lines," Schultz recalled in his memoir, *Onward*.[23] Schultz knew that management needed to focus on the barista and the store manager, since they interacted with the customer most. If management could put partner development first, the partners would take care of their customers. So early in the turnaround effort, Schultz and management focused on meeting partner needs through two programs. The first was to retrain all baristas on how to pour the perfect espresso. Starbucks temporarily closed all US stores for a day — on February 26, 2008, and at the cost of millions of dollars in lost revenue and even a dip in the stock price — to spend the time ensuring that its partners were refocused on the art of making coffee. The second program was a three-day Starbucks Leadership Conference to reengage store managers and demonstrate the company's rededicated commitment to them.

As we've seen in the research, store managers have a significant effect on how well the service-profit chain works to deliver customer loyalty and company growth. Starbucks sent 10,000 managers to New Orleans at a cost of $30 million. The scheduled events helped the store managers review the company's core values and learn about new technologies to make their jobs better; they also participated in team-building activities, including a daylong volunteer project serving the residents of New Orleans, who were still recovering from Hurricane Katrina. Overall, the partners were reassured that their role was absolutely central to the Starbucks customer experience.

One more gesture was central to reaffirming the company's commitment to its partners. Despite its steep cost — upward of $300 million per year — Schultz refused to cut the benefits plan, including health insurance for part-time workers. Schultz remained firm that honoring this commitment was the right thing to do, and that it was a part of the overall commitment to putting partners first. During the turnaround, Schultz faced a lot of pressure to cut health care, including personal phone calls from major stockholders telling him that no one would criticize him if he cut health insurance.

"I could cut $300 million out of a lot of things, but do you want to kill the company, and kill the trust this company stands for?" Schultz answered those who were concerned about health care costs.[24] Schultz told those who were concerned that his position would hurt the company's financial performance that perhaps they should sell their stock. Even when it came to issues like shareholder value, Schultz believed in creating value for employees first. "I do not believe that shareholder value is sustainable if you are not creating value for the people who are doing the work," he said.[25]

And over time the people doing the work at Starbucks created value for the company. By refocusing on serving the partners and then trusting them to serve customers, Schultz saw Starbucks begin to turn around. Despite some tough times and some serious questions from partners about Schultz's plan, morale began to improve — and service along with it. By 2009 new earnings were positive for the first time in two years.[26] The company had completed its turnaround and was moving forward. In the 2014 fiscal year, Starbucks earned $16.4 billion.[27] Or perhaps it's more appropriate to say that Starbucks's partners earned $16.4 billion for the company that invested in them and for the leader who quit the company twice but always returned to put partners first.

The belief shared by Vineet Nayar, Danny Meyer, and Howard Schultz that hierarchies ought to be flipped and customers put second is simple in theory, but in truth, it's not easy to put into practice. Most people have heard the old maxim that "the customer is always right" too many times to be able to accept a sudden flip like this. Turning the organization around requires turning loyalties around. These leaders demonstrated that their loyalty was to employees first, trusting that their employees would then be more loyal and caring to their customers. It was a big gamble, to be sure, but the results certainly speak for themselves.

3

■

LOSE THE STANDARD
VACATION POLICY

Many leaders are beginning to question why, in offices that do not
track hours worked, they need to track days not worked. Companies that have switched to unlimited vacation have found that
their old policies often limited employees' engagement and performance.

W HEN A COMPANY goes public, a lot of things change.
Shifting the availability of ownership shares from the
founders, venture capitalists, and a handful of accredited investors
to anyone and everyone who wants to buy shares through a public
stock exchange entails a great deal of regulatory work that yields
changes throughout every part of the company. All that being said,
when Netflix went public in 2002, company leaders weren't expecting to end up changing their long-standing vacation policy.[1]
Before it went public, Netflix's vacation policy functioned like the
policies at the majority of companies: you get a certain number of
vacation days per year, and any days left over you lose, roll over,

or get paid extra for at the end of the year. This kind of vacation policy is largely a holdover from the industrial age, when factory managers needed to ensure that all shifts were properly covered.

At Netflix, people received ten vacation days, ten floating holidays, and a few sick days. Employees were on the honor system, keeping track of the days they took off and letting their managers know when and how many they took. Freedom and responsibility are strongly valued in the Netflix culture, but after going public, culture and regulations collided in a number of ways. The first collision was instigated by the company's auditors, who claimed that Sarbanes-Oxley rules for public companies required Netflix to account for all time off taken by employees and that the honor system was an inadequate tracking system.

Meanwhile, a Netflix employee pointed out to the company's founder, Reed Hastings, that most people weren't working standard nine-to-five hours, or even the standard five days a week.[2] Instead, different employees worked different hours. Many worked nights or weekends and answered emails at odd hours of the day. Netflix had never asked employees to track the days they worked, the employee pointed out, so why was it now asking them to track the days they did not work? The traditional rationale — that shifts needed to be covered — just didn't apply to them.

So when regulators insisted to Hastings that Netflix formalize its vacation system, Hastings's mind took a different direction. "Are companies *required* to give time off?" he asked.[3] After researching the issue, Hastings found that no laws in the company's home state of California governed how much vacation time salaried employees received or how they had to take vacation. So in 2004, Hastings and his senior leaders decided to make their system *less* formal. In fact, they decided to scrap their vacation policy all together. Now their vacation policy is that there is *no* vacation policy. Netflix employees take as much time as they feel they need and inform their manager when they'll be gone — but they don't track how many vacation days they take each year.

Hastings and his colleagues would later write a public statement about their culture and the vacation policy. In a 128-slide PowerPoint deck titled *Reference Guide on Our Freedom and Responsibility Culture,* Hastings and his team wrote: "We realized we should focus on what people get done, not on how many days they worked. Just as we don't have a 9 a.m. to 5 p.m. workday policy, we don't need a vacation policy."[4]

The company does provide some guidance on how to responsibly act in the absence of such a policy. For example, employees in accounting and finance are encouraged not to be gone around the time a fiscal quarter closed, because that's a busy time for the whole team. Any employee who wants more than thirty days off in a row needs to meet first with human resources. In addition, the senior leaders are encouraged to take long vacations and to let the company know about them. "No vacation policy doesn't mean no vacation," Hastings wrote.[5]

Netflix wants its employees to get a good rest when they're off work so that they can be reenergized when they return, but when they're at work, it also wants employees to know that the company trusts them and expects them to act responsibly. The policy of no vacation policy reinforces that. In fact, the policy has worked so well that Netflix has started removing or simplifying needless policies in other areas as well. In 2015, Netflix announced that new mothers and fathers would also benefit from unlimited parental leave, allowing them to take off, move to part-time, then to full-time, and even back to time off, as their situation dictated, all without needing to file for state or disability pay and all while being paid normally.[6]

Netflix leaders have also made the travel and expenses policy considerably shorter. Instead of dictating when and how money can be spent and will be reimbursed, they have written a simple five-word policy: "Act in Netflix's best interest."[7] As with vacation days, the idea is to expect adult behavior from employees, then deal with those who can't act like adults without burdening the majority. "If you create a clear expectation of responsible behavior, most employees will comply," said Patty McCord, Netflix's chief talent officer at the time of the changes.

Even better, McCord found that simplifying the expense policy actually reduced costs, since employees acted responsibly when trusted and extra fees weren't going to the corporate travel agencies that typically enforce such policies. "Over the years we learned that if we asked people to rely on logic and common sense instead of on formal policies, most of the time we would get better results, and at a lower cost," said McCord.[8] This is Netflix's core assertion in a nutshell: *when you give your employees trust and freedom to act responsibly, you don't need nearly as many policies.* Perhaps Hastings and McCord said it best in their culture slide deck: "There is also no clothing policy at Netflix, but no one comes to work naked."[9]

The culture slide deck and the policy of no vacation policy garnered Hastings and Netflix a lot of attention and an enthusiastic response. The slide deck itself was viewed over 11 million times and written about in newspapers across the globe. Sheryl Sandberg, a former Google senior leader and the COO of Facebook, called the deck the most important document ever to come out of Silicon Valley. But perhaps the most influential viewer of the slide deck was Sir Richard Branson, the billionaire founder of the Virgin Group conglomerate.

Branson first saw the slide deck after his daughter emailed an article about it to him. "Dad, check this out," Branson said his daughter wrote. "It would be a very Virgin thing to do."[10] Branson read the document for himself and loved the concept, especially since it was a way to eliminate or simplify the red tape that stifles so many companies. "It's always interesting to note how often the adjectives 'smart' and 'simple' describe the cleverest of innovations — well, this is surely one of the simplest and smartest initiatives I have heard of in a long time," he wrote in a blog post to the entire company and to the world.

In that post, he also announced that Virgin was going to experiment with the same "nonpolicy" at its corporate headquarters. The salaried employees at Virgin Group, in both the United Kingdom and the United States, can now take as much time off as they like, with no one tracking it. Although initially only 170 employees are affected, Branson expects the new policy to be rolled out throughout the Virgin Group conglomerate eventually. "Assuming it goes well," Branson wrote in the post, "we will encourage all our subsidiaries to follow suit, which will be incredibly exciting to watch." "Exciting" is a good word for it: counting all of Virgin's subsidiaries, the company has an estimated 50,000 employees worldwide.

It wasn't just billionaire founders of 50,000-person global brands that took note of Netflix's policy; it was also smaller entrepreneurs with Netflix-sized ambitions for their start-ups. Zac Carman, CEO of the Tulsa-based ConsumerAffairs, noticed as well. Carman purchased the web-based consumer news and advocacy firm in 2010 when it was just eight people dispersed across the globe. Under Carman's leadership, the company has grown to over ninety people.

Crucial to that rapid scaling was making sure that the culture was ready to grow quickly. "As we grew, we needed to help define culture," Carman explained. "Part of that was my switching from command and control to freedom, responsibility, and a high-performance mentality." For Carman, formal policies on issues like vacation time represented the culture he needed to leave behind.

"The first time I read Netflix's culture document, I understood how to put to words the type of culture I knew we needed in order to scale."[11]

Offering an unlimited vacation, or a vacation nonpolicy, was a step toward building what Carman wanted — a culture of trust and freedom that would enable employees to focus on high performance. So Carman took the step and eliminated the traditional vacation policy and the control culture he felt it represented. ConsumerAffairs employees could take as much vacation as they wanted, so long as they worked with their managers to ensure that not too many people were all gone from work at a critical time. "And it worked," he said.

Carman now views such nonpolicies as part of building a high-performance culture in that they signal to employees and managers that the team needs to stay high-quality *because* of the freedom in these policies. "In many cases, companies that create a command-and-control system end up far less disciplined about hiring quality people. You don't need to trust them because you've got a policy to reinforce the behavior that you want." But when you do trust employees to be responsible about taking time off from work, as Carman, Branson, and Hastings have all found, they end up bringing quality performance to their time at work.

It's Not About Giving Days Off

One word commonly used by leaders who advocate vacation nonpolicies is "trust." Adopting such practices signals that they're placing greater trust in their employees. The hope is that those employees will positively respond to that trust. But the concept of trust is exactly what makes decisions like having no vacation policy seem vague and ambiguous. How can you quantify and analyze trust? We might not know how to mathematically quantify trust, but we may very well know how to describe it scientifically. Trust, it turns out, might be a chemical.

That chemical is called oxytocin.[12] Oxytocin is a peptide chain of nine amino acids (also called a nano-peptide) that is often called the "bonding hormone" because it is most present in humans when mothers give birth to and nurse their babies. Touching, bathing, and eating are also known to raise oxytocin levels. When it's secreted by the pituitary gland, oxytocin rushes to the brain and fills the synapses between neurons, creating a feeling of bliss and well-being that lasts for around five minutes. The feeling reduces heart rate, lowers respiration, and decreases stress hormones, and it also reduces the connectivity of the upper parts of the brain to the amygdala, famous for triggering the fight-or-flight response. In addition, oxytocin influences our brain's attention, memory, and ability to identify errors in the environment, all of which cascade into our decision-making process. For these reasons, many scientists theorize that oxytocin not only reduces fear but also produces trust between individuals.

Oxytocin's role in establishing trust and its effect on key decisions that are made once trust is established caught the attention of Paul Zak.[13] Zak is an adjunct professor of neurology at Loma Linda University's medical school, a professor of economics at Claremont Graduate University, and the director of Claremont's Center for Neuroeconomics Studies. Neuroeconomics is an emerging field that studies human decision-making through the lens of traditional economics but also through the scientific study of the brain. Naturally, the connection between oxytocin and decision-making would appeal to a researcher like Zak.

To study this connection, Zak conducted a slightly modified version of a long-standing research study in economics, the "investment game." (It's called a game because it is used mostly by researchers in the subdiscipline of economic game theory.) In a basic version of the investment game, two participants are randomly and anonymously partnered together, placed in separate rooms, and given a computer terminal with which to communicate. The participants in the first group (DM1) are then given $10 and told that they can send any amount between zero and $10 to their partner (DM2). They're also told that whatever amount they send to their partner will be tripled. So if DM1 sends $5 to DM2, DM2 will actually receive $15.

Participants in the second group (DM2) are told that they can give any amount of money (again including zero) back to their partners (DM1). This tripling and return is why the experiment is often called the investment game, as DM1 is investing in DM2 and hoping for a positive return. The game also measures trust, which standard economic theory predicts should be zero — the participants have never met, will never meet, and have no reason to trust each other. Strictly from a logical perspective, economic theory predicts that DM1 will not send money to DM2. After all, it's in DM2's best interest to keep the money, and so DM1 should anticipate this, send no money, and walk away with $10. Both parties should act in their own self-interest and try to maximize their gains.

But ironically, that's not what happens. In most studies based on the investment game, around 50 percent of DM1s decide to invest in their partner and send some amount of money over to them. Among the DM2s who receive the money, around 75 percent choose to reciprocate. For a long time this behavior baffled economists, who found it totally illogical. Zak wondered, however, whether the act of sending money was an act of trust and set out to measure whether that was the case. In Zak's version of the investment game, after participants were finished with the exchange, they were escorted down the hall and blood was drawn from their arm. Zak and his team processed each participant's blood to measure several different hormone levels, including oxytocin. Amazingly, Zak found that the oxytocin levels in the participants' blood correlated with their decisions in the investment game. In other words, the more money DM2s received from their partner, the more their oxytocin levels rose. "Oxytocin rises when someone trusts you," Zak explained, "and facilitates trustworthiness."[14]

Being trusted and subsequently experiencing heightened levels of oxytocin triggers in humans a more generous and more trusting response. When a person signals to you that he trusts you, you respond more positively. Moreover, because oxytocin affects the areas of the brain associated with memory, Zak theorizes, the brain may create more powerful memories of trusting behavior, and these memories may stimulate more trusting responses over extended periods of time. In short, trust breeds more trustworthy behavior.

Zak recommends that even more companies adopt programs and policies based on trust. "If these programs raise the set-point for oxytocin, then trust and productivity will increase when employees are at work," he wrote.[15] One such trust-based program is an unlimited vacation policy or a vacation nonpolicy. In simplifying their vacation policies and making them all about trust rather than a mere economic exchange of paid time off, company leaders like Hastings, Branson, and Carman all signaled to their employees that they trusted them. And their employees responded in kind.

Implementing a Nonpolicy

Trust even becomes the determining factor when an unlimited vacation policy does *not* work, as can be seen in those instances where leaders have tried and failed to implement a vacation non-policy.

In 2014 Tribune Publishing, the parent company of newspapers such as the *Chicago Tribune* and the *Los Angeles Times*, tried to implement an unlimited vacation policy.[16] Leaders at the company announced that, like Richard Branson, it would be adopting Netflix's vacation nonpolicy. They said that the company would be transitioning from a traditional policy of earning and banking vacation days — employees earned a fixed amount every year and were paid for days not taken — to what was labeled "Discretionary Time Off (DTO)."

However, it didn't go so well for Tribune: within a week the company had canceled its plan to adopt the new policy. Here's what happened: On November 13, a memo was circulated to all managers announcing the policy and outlining how it would work. The top of the memo was rich with the language of freedom, trust, and responsibility, but deep down in the memo was one line that stood out to the employees who eventually got a hold of the letter:

> All remaining unused vacation time earned or accrued under any former Tribune policy will be applied to employee absences until the accrual has been exhausted.[17]

That one line made a world of difference to employees at the *Los Angeles Times,* who spoke up in anger and threatened to sue the company.

Instead of moving to a purely unlimited policy covering time off, for the whole company at once, Tribune was instead telling employees that they would get as much discretionary time off as they would like once they'd exhausted their bank of already earned vacation days. Traditionally, these days would have been paid for, and employees felt that they should have been paid for at the time of the switch.

That simple addition to the policy positioned the change not as an act of trust but as a simple economic exchange. Where trust isn't present, the exchange becomes simply about maximizing your own gains at the expense of your partner. Employees at the *LA Times* clearly saw it as such and revolted against what they perceived as Tribune Publishing trying to steal their hard-earned vacation days. It's impossible to know whether Tribune's leaders were acting in trust or merely trying to eliminate the debt of unpaid vacation days from their books. Regardless, a few days into the revolt Tribune's head of human resources released another memo emphasizing the company's desire to adopt a policy "in the spirit" of the one at Netflix, but the memo reiterated that employees would have to use up their supply of already earned vacation days before switching to the unlimited vacation policy.[18]

On November 21, just eight days after announcing the original intended policy change, Tribune CEO Jack Griffin released a new memo stating that the company had reversed its decision. Griffin said that because the policy had "created confusion and concern within the Company," they would continue to operate as they always had. "Based on valuable input from employees," Griffin wrote, "the DTO policy is rescinded." To his credit, Griffin did mention that in making future decisions of this nature, he and Tribune's senior leaders would seek more and better input from everyone in the company. However, he didn't mention the core reason why *Times* employees were so upset: the lost vacation days.

In sum, the employees' trust that the company was acting in their interest was broken. Just like the examples of successfully implemented unlimited vacation policies, the example of failure at the Tribune reinforces the importance of using the policy to signal trust. When such a policy comes across as an attempt to take something away from employees, it will be seen as a violation of trust. However, when the adoption of a nonpolicy is seen as an investment of trust, the return on investment is significant and hugely positive.

That return even extends to trust between peers in the organization. Since 2011, the 300 non-unionized employees of Windsor Regional Hospital in Ontario, Canada, have been operating under an unlimited vacation policy, and it's been a success for the relationships not only between employees and senior leaders but also between employees and other employees.[19] Windsor Regional adopted the policy for two reasons: employees were not taking enough time off, and vacation days had begun to block recruiting efforts — the hospital could offer new employees only limited benefits because they feared upsetting longer-tenured employees.

David Musyj, the CEO of the hospital, and other senior leaders saw unlimited vacation as an opportunity to overcome those challenges and create a more engaged and trusting organization. When it was first announced, the policy was met with some skepticism. Some employees feared that they would lose their vacation time, while others feared that the policy just wouldn't work. A tech company in Silicon Valley is one thing, but a hospital that depends on having the right number of specialized employees staffed on every shift is a lot more complex. Musyj and his team worked to allay these fears and emphasized that the intent was to get employees to take more vacation and to work with each other to make sure everyone was supported when they were working. And it worked.

The staff of the hospital rested more when they took time off and engaged more when they were back on the job. "The energy they return to work with after being able to participate with their family is truly priceless for our patients," said Musyj.[20] Hospital staff also cooperate more with each other on the job. They've learned to collaborate on setting schedules and to pitch in during a colleague's absence. In the past, a coworker taking time off was often seen in a purely negative light, as creating a hole that other employees were obliged to fill. Now, however, keeping the hospital running is seen as a team effort ... and that sense of teamwork has affected more than just setting schedules. "These collaborative efforts have extended to day to day work activities," said Musyj, "resulting in a far more collegial workplace."

The policy has also benefited the hospital's recruiting and kept turnover to a minimum — resulting in loyal and engaged staff. "When I started with this organization," Musyj recalled, "... there was a handful of 'go-to' people. That list has since grown into the hundreds; there is always someone to turn to when something needs to get done." Musyj and his leadership team saw the unlimited vacation policy as a way not only to encourage employees to rest but also to signal their trust in employees. Windsor Regional employees, in turn, learned not only to trust Musyj more but to trust and collaborate with each other more.

Netflix, Virgin Group, ConsumerAffairs, and Windsor Regional are all very different organizations, but their differences actually disarm the most common objection to an unlimited vacation policy: "It won't work here." Their experiences suggest that such nonpolicies can work anywhere — anywhere employees are burned out or burdened by red tape. Anywhere high performers are desperate for simplicity and freedom and willing to be responsible in return is a candidate for nonpolicies.

Many leaders, however, looking at examples like the backlash at Tribune Publishing and feeling uncertain about what would happen once employees are given unlimited vacation, refrain from taking the leap. They find themselves in the position of DM1 in one of Paul Zak's studies — debating whether or not to hand over control to someone else. Trust, in the words of Zak, is "a tangible, intentional act in which you cede power over resources to another person."[21] By deciding to adopt unlimited vacation, Reed Hastings, Sir Richard Branson, Zac Carman, David Musyj, and other leaders decided to give up power so that their employees could gain autonomy. That decision paid off. And they learned that unlimited vacation isn't about days off.

It's about trust.

4

■

PAY PEOPLE TO QUIT

Helping employees quit, and literally paying them a quitting bonus, may seem insane, but many leaders are finding it worthwhile. Research suggests that such incentives might have a
positive effect on company performance — and even on the employees who stay.

At some point during their first weeks working at Zappos,
everyone gets "the offer."

It's an offer that has become legendary around the online re-
tailer, and it's not what you're thinking. It's the inverse of the offer
most of us get from an employer — the offer of a job. Instead, during their primary training at Zappos, new employees are offered
$4,000 to leave the company right then. They are paid *to quit*.

Four thousand dollars is a significant amount of money when
you figure that most of Zappos's 1,500-plus employees work in the
call center or in a company warehouse. For some, $4,000 is more
money than they'd make in a month if they stayed. But the offer is

there for the taking — it's scripted into every employee's onboarding process.

For new Zappos employees, the initial training is largely the same regardless of position. New hires spend their first four weeks in basic training, five days a week, from 7:00 a.m. to 4:00 p.m., with most of that time spent in the call center.[1] Regardless of where the new hires are headed, the company wants to make sure that all of them get the message that customer service is their number-one priority. So every new hire spends time on the phones and interacts with call center employees. During this time the company training also reinforces the company's unique culture and core values. And then, in week three, a trainer for the company makes them the offer: $4,000 if they decide that day that they don't want to be a part of the company.

Four thousand dollars. No questions asked. No counteroffer. "It's really putting the employee in the position of 'Do you care more about money or do you care more about this culture and the company?'" said Zappos CEO Tony Hsieh about the goal of the offer. "And if they care more about the easy money then we probably aren't the right fit for them."[2] In fact, Hsieh has gone to great lengths to make sure the offer is seen as easy money. When the offer started, it was a modest $100, but they found that not enough people were accepting it. So it was raised to $1,000, then $2,000, then $3,000, before it was ultimately pegged at where it is now, roughly one month's salary for an entry-level employee. It was an experiment to see how many people would take it each time the offer went up. Still, even at $4,000, few people accept the offer.

Zappos was founded in 1999 and within the first ten years grew to a company with $1 billion in revenue.[3] The company was the brainchild, not of Tony Hsieh, but of Nick Swinmurn, who as a twenty-six-year-old marketing manager at another online company was frustrated at how complicated finding the right pair of shoes had become. He launched Zappos originally as ShoeSite .com, but quickly donned the new name, a derivative of *zapatos*, the Spanish word for shoes. By January 2000, the company had sold more than 100 brands of shoes in a variety of styles. To scale more quickly, Swinmurn took on a $1.1 million investment from Tony Hsieh and his business partner Alfred Lin (who would become Zappos's CFO until 2010). Hsieh first became co-CEO with Swinmurn, then sole CEO in 2003 (with Swinmurn as chairman).

From the start, Hsieh focused on building a company where the culture was about customer service, but also about enjoying the work itself. Hsieh had gone through a series of past experiences that underscored the purpose of culture. Venture Frogs, the venture capital firm Hsieh and Lin cofounded, was funded by their previous business, LinkExchange, an Internet advertising company. Hsieh and Lin had scaled LinkExchange quickly, but made some sacrifices along the way. "As we grew beyond 25 people, we made the mistake of hiring people who were joining the company for other reasons," Hsieh recalled. "The good news was that the people we hired were smart and motivated. The bad news was that many of them were motivated by the prospect of either making a lot of money or building their careers and resumes."[4] And LinkExchange did make a lot of money.

The duo sold LinkExchange to Microsoft for $265 million in 1998. As part of the deal, Hsieh would receive $40 million if he stayed at the helm for longer than a year, but only 80 percent of that if he walked away beforehand.[5] Hsieh disliked the culture and loathed showing up for work every day, so he decided to pass on the extra millions and left. His departure paved the way for Venture Frogs and eventually for becoming the leader of Zappos, with its strong commitment to culture. His departure paid off.

In leading Zappos, Hsieh is committed to building a culture

that is dedicated to customers but is also fun and a little quirky. Zappos relies on this culture to grow its revenue. It does limited advertising but really doesn't need to: 75 percent of its revenue comes from repeat customers. Zappos isn't even the cheapest place to buy shoes, but it offers customers delightful experiences. For example, Zappos usually promises free four-day shipping to customers, then surprises them by shipping items overnight. Instead of cutting customer service calls short, Zappos employees take as long as needed, and if a particular item is out of stock, a Zappos employee will check three competitive websites to try to find the item for the customer. That kind of customer commitment is fueled by employees who are fully committed to a culture of service and committed to Zappos.

That culture begins at hiring. The company is specific about the core values that shape its culture and built its hiring process around that culture. But unlike many companies whose core values read like a list of vague generalities thought up by senior leaders during a company off-site, Zappos has core values that reflect the culture as it is, compiled after Hsieh facilitated a companywide search for them.[6] He surveyed all employees and developed a first-draft list of thirty-seven statements. Those statements were sent out for employee feedback, and eventually a list of ten core statements emerged.

The statements aren't vague either. Number one is "deliver wow through service"; number three is "create fun and a little weirdness." These core values are the basis for questions in one of two interviews that all new employees go through. In addition to an interview focused on skills and competencies, all candidates also undergo an interview designed to assess how well they align with Zappos's core values. "We have actually passed on hiring a lot of really talented people that we knew could make an immediate impact on the top or bottom line," Hsieh said. "But if they're not a cultural fit, we won't hire them."[7] Zappos's process for finding the right people to hire is one of the reasons so few people take the cash offered during training. If the interview process works properly, then few people will decide it's not a good fit.

That commitment to finding the right fit has paid off. In addition to loyal customers, it has also created loyal employees. As the company grew, it took on additional investment, and after an investment of $35 million from Sequoia Capital, Zappos migrated its headquarters and call center from San Francisco to Las Vegas.[8] As a testament to the strength of the Zappos culture, when the company moved, around 80 percent of its California-based employees moved with them.[9] When it first appeared on *Fortune*'s list of the best places to work, Zappos was already in the Top 25. It has even ranked as high as sixth.

In the call center industry, turnover rates average 150 percent; Zappos's call center turnover rate (including turnover due to promotion) averages less than one-third of that—an astonishing retention rate for a company that tries to bribe its new hires into leaving.[10] Equally astonishing is how quickly Zappos has grown. Ten years after its founding, the company was purchased by Amazon for $800 million. One of the primary requirements of the deal was that Amazon allow Zappos to function independently, a move intended to keep Zappos's culture untouched . . . even "the offer" remained after the buyout. And for good reason: the offer has been a core part of building the culture that built the company's value.

Two Good Reasons for Having Bonuses to Quit

Paying people to quit works in two different ways. The first is obvious: it screens out some people who would probably end up quitting anyway. In a purely logical world, as soon as people figure out that they have made a bad decision in coming to work at a company—whether it's Zappos or any other company—they would leave. However, we are not purely logical creatures. As such, we're all subject to a cognitive glitch that makes it difficult to quit the things we start. Economists often refer to this as the "sunk costs fallacy."[11] Sunk costs represent the time, money, or effort we've already invested in a course of action. Sunk costs have already been spent, and there's no getting them back whether we continue down the same course or break away and go our separate way.

Rationally, then, the moment we realize we've made a mistake, we should change our course of action. But we don't do that. In one of the original studies on sunk costs, Hal Arkes and Catherine Blumer (both of Ohio University at the time) asked undergraduate students to envision the following scenario and make a choice:

> Assume that you have spent $100 on a ticket for a weekend ski trip to Michigan. Several weeks later you buy a $50 ticket for a weekend ski trip to Wisconsin. You think you will enjoy the Wisconsin ski trip more than the Michigan ski trip. As you are putting your just-purchased Wisconsin ski trip ticket in your wallet, you notice that the Michigan ski trip and the Wisconsin ski trip are for the same weekend! It's too late to sell either ticket, and you cannot return either one. You must use one ticket and not the other. Which ski trip will you go on?[12]

Surprisingly, the majority of students picked the more expensive ticket. They opted for the Michigan trip even though the Wisconsin trip would be more fun. Despite the fact that the full $150 was spent and couldn't be recouped, the two researchers theorized, students were influenced by how much had been spent on the trip and that influence led them to pick a less enjoyable trip. Arkes and Blumer conducted four similar experiments, and since they published their research in 1985, other researchers have continuously replicated their findings. We're biased toward throwing more money or more effort at a less enjoyable — or outright doomed — cause if we've put significant effort or money behind it already. And jobs are no different.

It takes time to find a job, to search for openings and go on interviews, and when you're hired the hard work of training begins. Midway through training, if you realize that the job isn't right for you, your sunk costs put a lot of pressure on you to ignore that realization and just continue on. Offering a quitting bonus can help offset the sunk costs building up in the mind of the future underperformer. Likewise, companies invest a lot of money in finding and training new hires. It's safe to assume that, by the time Zappos makes you a $4,000 offer to quit, they've invested far more than that in recruiting and training you.

For both the employee and the employer, sunk costs make it difficult to end a doomed relationship. Offering to pay people to quit can alleviate some of that burden. Companies that pay people to quit are acting rationally and ignoring sunk costs. They realize that they can't really head off a future problem by investing more time and money in a person who isn't a good fit. When a company offers money to an employee to quit, it's often doing so in the belief that even if the employee accepts the offer, the company is getting a good deal. By giving the employees most likely to be disengaged the option to self-select out, companies save a lot in the long run. According to research from the Gallup Organization, disengaged employees are less productive, more likely to steal from their employer, more likely to skip work, and negatively influence customers and other employees.[13]

At Zappos, only 2 to 3 percent of people who get the offer take the offer. So what happens to everyone who stays? The answer to that question points to the second reason why paying people to quit works. Not only does the company get to keep the money when new employees turn down the offer, but they might even get a more engaged and productive employee than if they'd never made the offer. When this happens, another psychological phenomenon has come into play: cognitive dissonance.

"Cognitive dissonance" is the term psychologists use to describe the discomfort you feel when two ideas conflict in your mind, as well as your attempts to somehow reconcile the two ideas. The theory of cognitive dissonance was first proposed by Leon Festinger, a social psychologist who worked at a variety of universities, from MIT to Stanford. In his 1956 book *When Prophecy Fails*, Festinger attempted to explain the deep faith of cult members, even when prophecies espoused by cult leaders were obviously erroneous.[14]

Festinger detailed a particular cult whose members believed that a UFO would save them from the Earth's imminent destruction by shuttling true believers away to a new world. When the cult members gave away all their possessions and met at a certain place and time to await the ship's landing, but the aliens never arrived, they faced cognitive dissonance. Most resolved the dilemma by constructing a new storyline: the aliens had given Earth a second chance. Thus, the believers grew even stronger in their faith, despite the failed prophecy.

While this first explanation of cognitive dissonance may seem out of this world, later studies would expand the theory and demonstrate how we experience dissonance closer to home. Jack Brehm, another social psychologist, built on Festinger's theory with a phenomenon he labeled "post-decision dissonance." Brehm theorized that, after we make certain decisions, we modify our beliefs to strengthen the validity of that decision.

In a famous experiment, Brehm asked 225 female students to rate a series of common household appliances.[15] The students were then asked to choose between two of the appliances they'd rated to take home as a gift for participating. Brehm followed up with the students and asked them to complete a second round of rating the same appliances. Oddly, the students' ratings had changed. In the second round, most of the participants rated the appliance they'd chosen as a gift higher than they'd rated it in the first round, and likewise rated the rejected item lower than they had before.

Brehm argued that the students had experienced cognitive dissonance: in their attempt to resolve that dissonance in their minds, they'd adjusted their opinions of the two items to make the rejected item less preferred and the chosen item more desirable. When we experience dissonance after making a decision, we adjust our beliefs to validate our decision.

Post-decision dissonance can also affect our decision to accept a job offer — or to reject an offer to quit. "If you act a certain way, over time, you're going to overly justify your behavior," explained Dan Ariely, a behavioral economist at Duke University and author of *Predictably Irrational*. "So the next morning after you rejected the $4,000, you're going to wake up and say, 'My goodness, I really must love this company if I rejected all that money.'"[16] By giving the offer to its new hires after training, Zappos not only is giving potentially disengaged employees a chance to leave before they cause damage but may also be increasing the full engagement of the employees who stay. The rejected offer signals to both the company and the employee that he or she views the job as valuable and is fully committed and engaged.

Employees' rejection of the offer is also likely to be a strong driver of Zappos's low turnover rate. Why quit for free when you could have quit a few months ago for $4,000? Likewise, the offer is a strong driver of employee engagement. Engaged employees deliver everything the disengaged do not: they are more productive, more reliable, and more likely to have positive interactions with customers and coworkers that further the productivity and profitability of the company.[17] Zappos gets the best of all possible options from the majority of Zappos employees — the ones who rejected the offer. Not only does the company get to keep the $4,000, but it gets a better employee too.

Quitting Bonuses Are Rising

When Amazon acquired Zappos, it also acquired "the offer." In his 2014 annual letter to shareholders, Amazon founder Jeff Bezos explained that the company had added a new program modeled after the one started by Tony Hsieh. After tweaking it a bit, Bezos and Amazon aptly titled the program "Pay to Quit."[18]

The program works differently than at Zappos. Rather than receiving the offer once during primary training, employees at Amazon's fulfillment centers get the offer once a year, every year. And the quitting bonus gets bigger every year. In the first year the offer is extended the amount is $2,000. Every year thereafter it goes up by $1,000 until it reaches $5,000, where it stays every year thereafter. Amazon raised the stakes of the quitting bonus above Zappos's level to better align it with the idea of the sunk costs fallacy.

Each year an employee gets the offer he or she has invested more in the company, and hence it might be harder to walk away, so the offer gets bigger to adjust to the increasing sunk costs. (By the way, Amazon's offer is only extended to fulfillment center workers — the lower-wage employees who run around large warehouses to collect items, package them, and ship them.) For shareholders who might think that paying $5,000 to an hourly employee who decides to quit is a waste of money, Bezos explained the rationale: "The goal is to encourage folks to take a moment and think about what they really want," he wrote. "In the long-run, an employee staying somewhere they don't want to be isn't healthy for the employee or the company."[19]

Like Hsieh, Bezos understands that disengaged employees impose financial and emotional costs on an organization, and that even offering $5,000 to help such employees self-select out of the company is a good deal. The real upgrade that Amazon made in the Pay to Quit program over the Zappos program was checking in further along in an employee's tenure and doing so more than just once. In a way, Amazon is asking its employees to give the company a performance evaluation every year.[20] But just as at Zappos, only a small number of employees take the offer — suggesting that employees are giving the company a pretty good evaluation.

One reason could be the effect of post-decision dissonance. Just as at Zappos, rejecting the offer strengthens Amazon employees' belief that the company is a great place to work — otherwise, why wouldn't they have taken the exit cash? But unlike Zappos employees, Amazon employees are asked to make this decision once a year, and so their post-decision dissonance is refreshed every time. Hence, Amazon achieves the most desired scenario: employees stay engaged, and the effect of their engagement on their productivity lasts longer.

Like Hsieh, Bezos wants employees to stay with the company and to be further engaged more than he wants them to quit. In fact, the title of the page that employees read when they receive the offer is "Please Don't Take This Offer." In making the offer every year, Bezos and Amazon achieve greater engagement and productivity, and they rarely even have to pay out $5,000. That's a good deal for all the shareholders, even the ones who might have read the letter skeptically. Gallup's research found that, in 2011–2012, publicly traded companies with 9.3 or more engaged employees for every disengaged employee had 147 percent higher earnings per share than their competitors. Meanwhile, companies with little engagement — 2.6 engaged employees for every disengaged employee — had 2 percent less earnings per share than competitors.[21]

Giving $5,000 to an exiting employee seems like a lot to pay, but one company has raised the stakes of the offer even further. Riot Games, the Santa Monica, California–based creator of the hugely popular video game "League of Legends," announced in 2014 that it would offer new employees up to $25,000 to quit.[22] Specifically, Riot Games offers new employees 10 percent of their annual salary (up to $25,000) if they quit within the first sixty days of their tenure, even if they quit on the very first day. The program, called "Queue Dodge," was influenced by Zappos's offer.

However, Riot Games employees aren't hourly call center workers; they're highly paid software engineers with salaries that can quickly get into six figures. But the spirit is the same. On the one hand, Riot Games leaders see paying 10 percent now to an employee who is going to disengage and eventually leave as a bargain compared to paying them for a year or more of poor performance and poor fit. "If someone gags on the unique flavor of our culture, they'd be doing themselves and the company a disservice to hang on just for the paycheck," the company explained in the blog post announcing the new program. "Rather than allow mismatches to fester, we want to resolve them quickly. This is good for the company, and good for the professional."

Like other quit bonuses, the Queue Dodge is an offer that the company is hoping will be rejected: "We don't want to actively push people out or dare them to leave, but we do want to provide a well-lit, safe exit path." The company is also hoping that the program serves as an engagement tool for the employees who don't take the offer. "Culturally aligned people and teams are more effective, and alignment around mission and values allows us to better serve players," they also wrote.

Whether offering $4,000 once hired, $5,000 every year, or $25,000 in the first two months, paying people to quit makes sense. Paying to quit works not only when employees accept the offer, self-select out, and do no further damage to a company's performance, but also when remaining employees are encouraged to value their job and engage with the company.

If offering cold, hard cash to quit still seems too far gone to be implemented at your firm, it's at least worth considering how the principles behind "the offer" can be used in other ways. Money isn't the only way to help employees offset the sunk costs that drive them to stay the course on a meaningless path. Indeed, any program that provides "a well-lit, safe exit path" would have a similar effect. Likewise, anything that encourages employees to examine or reexamine their reasons for choosing to work for your company is likely to encourage them to reaffirm the wisdom of their original decision, and hence to engage further with the organization. In other words, there is more than one way to extend "the offer." And the offer is a good deal.

5

■

MAKE SALARIES TRANSPARENT

While sharing salaries might raise privacy concerns, some leaders have found that keeping them secret might be hurting employees even more. Research suggests that pay secrecy actually lowers overall employee performance and produces more strife and distress in the workplace.

D ANE ATKINSON WASN'T always a champion of sharing salaries.

As a serial entrepreneur who started his first company at just seventeen years old, Atkinson used the secrecy of individual employee salaries to his advantage several times over. "I have been downright abusive; it's an abusive system. Many times I paid two people with the very same qualifications entirely different salaries, simply because I negotiated better with one person than another," said Atkinson, referring to how he leveraged salary secrets to pay as little as possible to get the talent he needed for his growing companies.[1]

"In past companies, when you're negotiating, you're always fishing for information. You want to get the candidate to reveal what they want first, so you ask them what they're expecting salary-wise or what they made in their past job. One person will say they made $80,000 and another person will say they made $50,000," Atkinson explained. "You would rarely tell the $50,000 person: 'Oh, that's insane. You should make seventy here, no problem.'

"Instead, you tell them you really like them and can probably get up to their number." To the person who made $80,000 in his last job, Atkinson would give a similar response. The end result? If both people are hired, his company has presumably acquired $160,000 in talent for only $130,000. For Atkinson, it was just a regular part of growing a company while saving on payroll, and it was hard *not* to do. "If you're working with investors," he rationalized, "undercompensation is a shareholder value tactic. If you can get talent at a discount, your board will cheer. That's why it's an abusive system."[2]

In most of the Western world, salary just isn't something people feel comfortable talking about. You're not supposed to flaunt how much you make to your neighbors, and you're definitely not supposed to flaunt your salary around the office. To many people, it's the polite and right thing to do to keep salaries a secret. It can even be seen as being done in the interest of respecting employees' privacy and looking out for their interests.

At the turn of the millennium, over one-third of American employers surveyed had implemented rules prohibiting employees from discussing salaries.[3] However, such policies were already being implemented eighty years earlier. In one famous example, the management of *Vanity Fair* magazine circulated a memo entitled "Forbidding Discussion Among Employees of Salary Received."[4] The memo didn't sit well with every employee. Famed writers Dorothy Parker and Robert Benchley, along with editor Robert Sherwood, responded the following day by arriving at the office with their salaries proudly written on signs hanging from their necks.

Their tactics may have been a little forward, but the trio may also have been ahead of their time. A significant number of thriving companies of all sizes are now making salaries public knowledge. A growing body of research suggests that keeping salary information from employees can actually damage employees' engagement, as well as their pocketbooks by keeping salaries below fair market rate. Not only that, but sharing salaries may even increase productivity.

While keeping salaries secret is commonplace in many organizations, the problems created by secrecy are also commonplace in economics. Secrecy leads to what economists call "information asymmetry," a situation in which one party in a negotiation has more or more accurate information than the other party has. Although both sides of a salary negotiation have access to privileged information (both the employer and the prospective employee know her old salary), the employer holds a much greater amount of privileged information (the salary of everyone in the company and the budget for the position) and is therefore able to gain an advantage in most situations. The problems of information asymmetry abound, everywhere from insurance sales to loan agreements and even to contract/salary negotiations. Information asymmetry can cause markets to go awry and sometimes can produce a total market failure.

The effects of information asymmetry are so great that the Nobel Prize in Economics was awarded in 2001 to the three economists who laid a foundation for understanding and combating the market problems it creates. George Akerlof, Michael Spence, and Joseph E. Stiglitz shared the prize for their "analyses of markets with information asymmetry."[5] Although they recommended several strategies for resolving asymmetry, they all had one thing in common: the need to share more information. The more openly information is shared, the more efficiently the market performs. This appears to be true whether you're buying a car or interviewing for a job.

Dane Atkinson didn't win a Nobel Prize, but his experience and solutions are in line with the insights of the now-famous economists who studied the problem in the 1970s. For Atkinson, the "market failure" was distraught coworkers becoming angry at each other and at the company when they found out how much their salaries differed from their peers' salaries. "At past companies, people would cry or scream at each other if they realized they had been undercompensated," he said. "It can cause a lot of strife. I've seen tears dropping from their eyes as they yelled and screamed at each other or at me."[6] For Atkinson, the pain of watching honest and talented employees degraded emotionally just wasn't worth the savings in unpaid salaries. So when he and his partners launched SumAll, a Manhattan-based data analytics company, they decided to try something different. Rather than keep employees in the dark about each other's salaries, they would instead be completely open.

When SumAll was launched, its ten employees started with totally transparent salaries, and that is still the case today. Each employee knows exactly what every other employee is being paid. When new employees join, they are assigned to one of nine salaries, all fixed based on the position.[7] The salaries range from around $35,000 to $160,000. Salary raises are tied to market conditions and to company performance. Every employee's name and corresponding salary is posted on the company's internal network, where any employee can view it at any time.

SumAll grew quickly and now employs over fifty people. For many of them, open salaries took some adjustment. Most employees are used to the double-blind negotiation process that most traditional corporations require. Instead, when SumAll managers make an offer, they basically say, "Here's what this position pays," and allow the potential new hire to accept it or turn it down, but the offer is fixed. "I often interview and make offers to people who expect to negotiate," said Atkinson. "Some of them are a little uncomfortable with the fact that they didn't have a chance to negotiate."[8]

Once employees accept the offer and start working on the inside, however, they see that sharing salaries is a way to make sure everything stays fair. If an employee looks at what he is paid compared to similar positions, then he can bring it up with his boss. If a new employee is brought on at a higher rate, older employees can have a conversation about it and find a fair resolution.

In fact, that exact situation has happened at SumAll. An engineer at SumAll was on a three-person panel to interview a new hire and discovered that the candidate was going to be offered more than he himself was making, despite having less experience. So the engineer brought it up to Atkinson and others, saying that he felt this wouldn't be fair. SumAll responded by raising his salary. "But if you're in a traditional system, you have no recourse," Atkinson said. "You could find out exactly what someone else makes and be distraught by it, but you can't address the issue because you're not supposed to know."[9]

Being able to have that open conversation is perhaps why SumAll team members find it so easy to stay with the company, even when other offers come to them. Atkinson said that SumAll employees regularly get offers from companies like Google and Facebook and turn them down because they'd rather work in SumAll's open salary culture.

Atkinson has become a champion of sorts for total salary openness. "We just want to be the counterpoint to the corporate culture that's out there," he said. "We want to help people understand that there are other ways to build successful organizations." And while sharing salaries is counterculture to most of the current corporate world, the practice is spreading. In 2013 the social media management company Buffer announced that it was diving into radical openness and sharing the salaries of employees not just with the company but with the whole world.

"We see no reason not to share everything," said Joel Gascoigne, the founder of Buffer.[10] In a blog post on the company's website, Gascoigne explained that transparency is a prominent ideal within Buffer's "Nine Values," and that the company is always looking to see how it can improve transparency.[11] Even before publishing salaries, Buffer openly shared its revenues and the number of its users with the public, as well as monthly progress reports. Inside the company, employees openly share their self-improvement plans with everyone, and every email sent between two people on the team is stored on an email list that anyone in the company can access. "One key reason transparency is such a powerful value for a company's culture is trust: Transparency breeds trust, and trust is the foundation of great teamwork."[12]

Applying the value of transparency to employees' pay seemed like the next logical step, so Buffer took it.[13] On December 19, 2013, Gascoigne posted a notice on the company's website about the new policy and listed all employees' salaries, including his own ($158,800) and even the salaries of the three people who were in the "bootcamp" trial period, who were technically freelancers awaiting a full-time offer ($70,000 to $94,000).[14] But Buffer took transparency one step further. In addition to publishing salaries, Buffer also published the formula for *how* each salary was calculated. Currently, that formula is as follows:

$$\text{Salary} = [\text{job type}] \times [\text{seniority}] \times [\text{experience}] + [\text{location}] + [\text{equity or \$10,000}]$$

For each category, there are variables, which currently comprise six job types, six seniority levels, four tiers of experience, and four categories of location based on cost of living. Thus, every employee is given not only a clear, logical formula that explains why she is paid what she is paid but also the opportunity to discuss whether or not she feels she is being paid fairly. Gascoigne meets with every employee once a month, and team leaders have biweekly one-to-one meetings in which progress, development, and compensation are all topics open for discussion.

It's difficult to know how well the formula will hold up as Buffer grows, but Gascoigne said that the company is always open to updating it based on changing circumstances and employee needs.[15] At the time salaries were made public, there were only fifteen people working at Buffer. What is clear, however, is that when Buffer does need to add more employees, it won't have a hard time finding people. In the month after making salaries public, Buffer received more than double the normal number of applications, going from 1,263 in the thirty days before Gascoigne's post went live to 2,886 in the thirty days afterward. Reporting that "we've never been able to find great people this quickly in the past," Gascoigne expected the company to grow to about fifty employees over the course of the year after salaries were made public.[16]

The Case for Sharing

The idea of total transparency in salaries isn't actually that new. For decades now, Whole Foods has allowed employees to look up performance data for departments and stores and the salaries of every employee in the company.[17] Founder John Mackey started the policy in 1986 after keeping salaries secret became more trouble than he felt it was worth. "I kept hearing from people who thought I was making too much money. Finally, I just said, 'Heck, here's what I'm making; . . . here's what everybody's making," Mackey said.[18] Salary information for civil service employees, as well as employees of large public organizations, is publicly available. And now the number of for-profit companies experimenting with sharing salaries is growing, and many, like SumAll and Buffer, are thriving because of it. But the for-profit sector isn't the only place where interest in sharing salaries is growing. Organizational psychologists and management researchers have recently been studying the effects of pay secrecy and sharing salaries, and the findings are as supportive of transparency as Buffer's deluge of job applications.

Researchers Elena Belogolovsky (Cornell University) and Peter Bamberger (Tel Aviv University) found that keeping salaries secret is associated with decreased employee performance.[19] They studied 280 Israeli undergraduate students, who were all paid a base salary for completing three rounds of a computer matching game with bonuses based on how well they played the game. Even though participants played the game individually, they were assigned to a four-person work group.

Half of the participants were given information about their performance and bonus pay alone (pay secrecy). The other half were given information about their own performance and their pay, but also the same information for the other three people in their work group (pay transparency); they knew what everyone else was getting paid. Members in every work group were given the opportunity to communicate with each other between rounds, but the pay secrecy group was restricted from discussing anything related to pay. In addition, some students were assigned to an absolute condition — pay was said to be linked to performance (how many matches) — while others were assigned to a relative condition — pay was said to be linked to performance *relative* to the performance of their work group (who had the most matches in the group).

When the research duo calculated all the performance data, they found that lack of transparency was associated with decreased performance. When students in the pay secrecy group were also told that their pay was relative to the performance of others (whose performance and pay they couldn't see), their performance was even worse. In addition, the high-performing participants were even more affected when they couldn't see a clear link between pay and performance among their entire work group.

So it's clear that keeping pay secret is related to disengagement and decreased performance. But can openly sharing pay information actually yield increases in performance? That's the question that Emiliano Huet-Vaughn, an assistant professor of economics at Middlebury College, sought to answer during his doctoral studies at the University of California at Berkeley. Huet-Vaughn designed an experiment to see if exposing people to information about their pay in relation to pay for others would trigger increases or decreases in the level of effort they put forth.[20] To do this, he first recruited over 2,000 people through Amazon's Mechanical Turk platform. This platform, often called MTurk, is commonly used for recruiting workers for small-scale tasks, and in research it can provide a sample more representative of the greater population than the undergraduate students typically recruited by many professors.

Participants were asked to complete two rounds of the data entry task of entering the correct bibliographic information for academic articles; they were paid a piece rate for each correct entry. At the end of the first round, some of the participants were shown their earnings and also the earnings of others performing the task, while others were given only their own earnings information. In the second round of work, participants who were shown their earnings relative to others worked harder and significantly increased their performance. The performance gains were especially great among those who were ranked high after the first round of work; high performers worked harder to stay high performers.

Taken together, these two studies suggest that not only does pay secrecy put a damper on individual performance, but also that revealing pay information can actually increase performance, especially among top performers. Although both of these studies are relatively recent, the theoretical foundation for both dates back to the 1960s and the research of John Stacey Adams, a workplace and behavioral psychologist who worked for General Electric.

Adams argued that employees have a strong desire to maintain equity between the inputs (performance) they bring to the work and the outputs (pay) that they receive from the organization as they relate to the perceived inputs and outputs of their coworkers.[21] To do this, employees are constantly seeking out information not just about their own performance and pay but also about the performance and pay ranges of their coworkers. This explains why employees, even if subtly, often try to glean pay and performance information from their peers — and why, on the rare occasion that people actually reveal what they're paid or someone accidentally leaves a pay stub on the copy machine, chaos ensues.

Adams labeled his assertion "equity theory" and proposed that employees who think they're under- or overpaid experience distress and will take actions to restore the perception of equity. When employees feel underpaid relative to their peers, their distress will most likely result in decreased performance as they lower their effort to bring their performance in line with their perceived rewards. This distress can also lead them to develop hostility toward the organization and toward their coworkers.

Equity theory explains the stress, shouts, and tears of many of

Dane Atkinson's former employees whenever new information about the pay of a coworker upset the perceived equity and fairness of the organization. In fact, in another experiment by Belogolovsky and Bamberger, the detrimental effects of pay secrecy were found to be highest in those with a low tolerance for perceived inequity.[22] Those who value fairness are most distressed when their perception of fairness is violated.

Compounding the challenges of equity theory and the perceptions of fairness is the fact that individuals are actually pretty terrible at comparing their salaries to the salaries of coworkers when the information isn't public. Edward Lawler, a business professor at the University of Southern California's Marshall School of Business, has been asking pay transparency questions for over five decades. In one study, Lawler found that employees who lack pay transparency often overestimate the salaries of people below them in the organizational chart and also underestimate the salaries of those higher up.[23]

So if our perceptions about others' pay are so skewed, how likely is it that our desire for fairness will be satisfied? Our desire for fairness (along with our inability to accurately assess salaries) makes Buffer's decision to share not just everyone's salary but also the formula for how those salaries are calculated so smart. It's possible to argue that the formula is unfair, but if everyone is subject to the same formula, then at least the ratio of contribution to salary is constant across the organization.

Beyond the psychological reasons that support sharing salaries, there are a host of potential legal reasons as well. In the United States, it wasn't until after she received an anonymous message about unfair pay that Lilly Ledbetter started challenging her company on the grounds of discrimination.[24] Ledbetter's case went all the way through the legal system and ended up in front of the Supreme Court. The Court famously rejected her claims based on the statute of limitations. However, the Court's decision became the basis for the first bill that Barack Obama signed into law as president, the Lilly Ledbetter Fair Pay Act of 2009, which dramatically extended the time allowed for employees to file discrimination claims.

But the success of such a law requires increased pay transparency. In a paper published in the *Penn State Law Review*, Gowri Ramachandran, an associate dean of research and professor of law at Southwestern Law School, proposes that pay transparency is the best remedy to address discrimination issues in the workplace.[25] Ramachandran proposes that sharing salaries is often the best treatment for a wide variety of pay discrimination symptoms. For example, according to a 2011 report from the Institute for Women's Policy Research, "the gender wage gap for all full-time workers, based on median annual earnings, is 23 percent. In the federal government, where pay rates are transparent and publicly available, the gender wage gap is only 11 percent."[26] Ramachandran even points to evidence that women and minorities gravitate toward organizations where salary information is shared, like Buffer and SumAll, and suggests that the reason is the more favorable compensation equality among comparable jobs.

Even with such strong evidence, Ramachandran knows that her assertion is counterintuitive and possibly uncomfortable. "Having one's salary exposed to one's colleagues is a scary prospect," she wrote. "But those who are employees should consider that the social awkwardness will often be made up for by higher pay, since employers who take advantage of the pay transparency defense will lose much of their information advantage in salary negotiation." For Ramachandran on the legal side, just as for Belogolovsky, Bamberger, and Huet-Vaughn on the psychological aspect, the core issue is always the perception of fairness and equity theory. Openness remains the best way to ensure fairness.

Too Much Sharing Too Soon?

Sharing salaries the way Dane Atkinson and Joel Gascoigne did is supported by the empirical evidence as well as by the theoretical and legal implications. However, recent research also suggests that jumping right to total transparency can result in chaos.

In 2008 a court ruling on California's "right to know" law opened up salary information for state employees. The *Sacramento Bee* newspaper published a website where users could search for the salary information of any state employee. This sudden and drastic act of transparency was studied by a team of researchers led by David Card of the University of California at Berkley.[27] Card and his team contacted a random group of employees from three University of California campuses and tipped them off as to the existence of the website. Several days later, the team surveyed all employees from the same campuses, asking about their pay, their job satisfaction, their intentions to look for another job, and, of course, their use of the website. When the research team analyzed the survey responses, they found that use of the website (and hence awareness of peer salaries) had an effect on job satisfaction and job search intentions, but the effect was asymmetric.

Those employees who used the website and found out that their salary was lower than the median for similar positions were more dissatisfied in their jobs and more likely to want to look for another job. Interestingly, Card and his team also found that differences in how one person's salary ranked among his or her peers had more of an effect than just the differences in pay levels. These results are in line with what Adams's equity theory predicts for when pay is perceived as unfair. "People who were told about the website were much more likely to use it, more likely to believe their wages were set unfairly and more likely to say they plan to look for another job," Card said of the study.[28] His team's results and equity theory's implications underscore the importance of making sure that pay is truly fair before pay is made transparent.

For example, before Buffer went public with its salary information, the company had to adjust each employee's salary to get it in line with the new formula. In the short term, this was costly. Every employee but one got a raise. In the early days of SumAll, new hires were announced via an email blast with the new team member's name, background, and salary. Although this method seemed like a good idea at first, it caused some minor frustrations as old employees read each email and wondered if the new hire would be worth the money. Eventually, they asked Atkinson to stop the emails about new employees. "They told me that every time we broadcast a new hire and a salary, they started spending too much time wondering whether or not the company was getting a good deal," he said. "It was a distraction."[29] So Atkinson stopped emailing new announcements and started adding new hires to the list instead. It took some tweaking, but SumAll arrived at a way to share salaries that had the benefits of transparency with few of the drawbacks. "Now the majority of people don't check the list regularly," he said. "Even for new hires, it's anticlimactic. You look everyone up at first, but it eventually becomes no big deal."[30]

John Mackey said that salary disagreements continue at Whole Foods, but that disagreements have a purpose and spur a deeper conversation about pay than he could imagine to have been possible if salaries were still a secret.[31] When people challenge him about a particular person's salary, comparing it to their own, he often responds, "That person is more valuable. If you accomplish what this person has accomplished, I'll pay you that too."

Joel Gascoigne also had to make some tweaks along the way, both to the formula and to actual salaries, and that is his recommendation to those looking to become more transparent with salaries. "Just do a little bit," he said. "Experiment with transparency in a small way. You don't have to go as far as posting everyone's salary on the blog."[32] Instead of posting salaries for the whole world to see, leaders can keep this information in-house, as SumAll did, or give employees the freedom to choose who knows. As a company experiments, learning what its employees like and what they find intolerable, it finds the path toward a transparency system designed around the needs, desires, and motivations of its employees.

Many companies don't share information about how they determine individual salaries, yet sharing that information alone can help restore a sense of fairness and equity to the minds of employees. Making the pay formula public was enough to eliminate some of the damaging effects of pay secrecy found in Belogolovsky and Bamberger's studies.

In addition, sharing where individuals fall within a range of salaries or compared to their peers (without sharing their peers' exact salaries) can leverage the benefits of transparency that Huet-Vaughn found in his research. When people know where they stand, and know how to move up in the range, they're more motivated to work to improve their performance and improve their standing.

Although total transparency may not be feasible for your company's culture, the evidence suggests that any steps taken toward transparency will improve perceptions of fairness and feelings of engagement — and ultimately boost performance in dramatic ways.

6

■

BAN NONCOMPETES

Putting noncompete clauses in employment contracts is a long-held practice. Evidence suggests, however, that noncompete clauses hurt not only departing employees but also those who stay with the company as well as the company itself. That's why more and more leaders are creating non-noncompete environments in which information is shared freely, even with outsiders.

T HE PAST FEW YEARS have been pretty good for noncompete clauses and the lawyers who write them and enforce them. Noncompete agreements, or noncompete clauses, are the agreements typically entered into when employees first join a new organization. The employees consent, if they leave the company, to not going to work for a rival or establishing a competing business for a fixed period of time.[1] What was once limited to engineers and senior managers in research and development-heavy industries is now seen in a wide variety of fields and in a wider variety of jobs — including a few where a noncompete clause would once have been completely unexpected.

In 2014, Cimarron Buser testified in front of Massachusetts state lawmakers about his nineteen-year-old daughter's surprising encounter with her first noncompete.[2] His daughter, Colette, found herself without a summer job when the camp she was planning to work for withdrew its offer at the last minute. The reason given was that Collette had worked the three previous summers at a LINX summer camp. Tucked into her contract with LINX was an agreement that forbade her from working at any competing camp within a ten-mile radius of any of LINX's thirty camps for one year.

Collette's potential new employer feared a lawsuit from LINX and so pulled its offer. At the hearing, Mr. Buser testified that neither he nor Colette had any idea they'd agreed to the noncompete, as well as about how ridiculous it seemed for a summer camp to restrict its former employees so rigidly. In an interview with the *New York Times,* LINX's founder and owner, Joe Kahn, defended putting the noncompete in his camp counselor contracts, calling it perfectly reasonable. "Our intellectual property is the training and fostering of our counselors, which makes for our unique environment," Kahn said. "It's much like a tech firm with designers who developed chips: You don't want those people walking out the door."

While comparing the contributions of a summer camp counselor to a computer engineer might seem like a stretch, some instances of noncompete clauses require even more flexibility. Training on how to grow and develop young minds might truly be intellectual property, but what about making a sandwich?

Also in 2014, employees of Jimmy John's Gourmet Sandwiches franchises filed a class action lawsuit accusing the company of a variety of ills.[3] The lawsuit was originally filed as a wage theft case — employees were being forced to work off the clock — but the filing was amended to include a complaint about Jimmy John's unreasonably broad and oppressive noncompete agreement. By signing the agreement, employees agreed not to work for or own an interest in any competitor located within a three-mile radius of any Jimmy John's store.

Jimmy John's held a very broad definition of "competitor." The agreement defined a competitor as "any business which derives more than ten percent (10%) of its revenue from selling submarine, hero-type, deli-style, pita and/or wrapped or rolled sandwiches."[4] Including any company that has even a minor revenue stream selling sandwiches is a wide label for a competitor — and even wider when we factor in that Jimmy John's has over 2,000 locations in the United States alone. The blackout area for former employees affected by this clause covers 6,000 square miles and forty-four states. It's worth noting that the agreement itself was upheld by the courts and that technically it is optional: it's left up to the individual store franchisee whether to include it in a hiring packet of documents.[5] Still, the desire to protect the intellectual property gained from low-wage sandwich makers who might migrate to another sandwich shop (or any business that sell sandwiches) seems a little out of place.

Not as out of place as inside a church.

In the Seattle area, also in 2014, one church came under fire and eventually was dissolved after several former members and former employees called for changes in the operation of the organization.[6] Mars Hill, a megachurch under the leadership of Mark Driscoll, was organized as a network of campuses with pastors serving at every campus. Those pastors, even the volunteer ones, were required to sign an agreement that included what was labeled a "Unity of Mission" but read an awful lot like a noncompete clause.

The agreement stated: "We commit that our next church ministry will not be within ten miles of any location of Mars Hill Church, except with the express consent of the local pastors of the nearest church, the sending church, if different, and the Executive Elders of Mars Hill Church." The agreement wasn't in the employment contract (since it applied to paid as well as unpaid pastors) but was part of an annual agreement signed every year by pastors, elders, and other volunteers. One pastor who volunteered his time to the church was removed from his position for declining to sign the agreement. The story of the noncompete and the dismissed pastor came to light during a larger questioning of Mars Hill's actions for operating too much like a cutthroat business and not enough like a church.

Later in the year, these challenges led Mark Driscoll to resign from the leadership of Mars Hill. The organization was dissolved, and each campus was turned over to its campus pastor to be run as an individual church or merged with another local church.[7]

While summer camps and sub sandwiches tested the flexibility of a noncompete clause, Mars Hill certainly brought it to the break-ing point. When Mars Hill's leadership redefined other churches as competitors and discouraged the launch of new churches, the Mars Hill community responded by discarding that definition and collaborating with those same churches.

The Mars Hill example isn't the first instance of rejection of a noncompete clause. In fact, the history of rejecting the validity of noncompete agreements is a pretty long one. The earliest known instance of a noncompete covenant being invoked was way back in 1414.[8] In that case, an English clothes dryer took his former worker to court, attempting to prevent the clothes worker from competing in the same town for six months.

The judge's decision didn't go so well for the clothes dryer or the noncompete. The court reprimanded the clothes dryer for bringing forth a frivolous lawsuit. It argued that the clothes dryer's request to restrict another citizen's right to work was an absurd restriction of trade. Not only was the case thrown out, but the clothes dryer was threatened with imprisonment for his misuse of the court. Fast-forward a few hundred years, however, and the dominant perspective on noncompetes has changed dramatically. Around 90 percent of managers and technical employees in the United States have signed a noncompete agreement.[9] Of those who have, nearly 70 percent report that they were asked to sign a noncompete after accepting a job offer, presumably when they had already turned down other offers and were left with few other options but to sign.[10]

Thus, the majority of people who sign noncompetes do so less than voluntarily. And courts tend to uphold the legitimacy of such clauses, except in one ironic area: the legal profession itself. The American Bar Association (ABA) continues to oppose noncompete agreements at law firms.[11] The ABA's rules ban noncompetes entirely. Their argument is that any restriction of a lawyer's ability to practice after leaving a firm is unethical and harmful, as it would limit lawyers' professional autonomy as well as clients' freedom to choose legal representation. The same lawyers who write and enforce noncompete agreements have consistently asserted that they themselves should be exempt from such covenants, for the good of the public.

How Noncompetes Affect Performance

The rationale behind noncompete agreements is that they are in the best interest of all parties. Without such agreements, the logic goes, organizations would have little incentive to spend time and money developing the skills of employees or investing in innovative research, since employees could easily depart and move to a rival at will. Since the employer's investment is protected, it makes that investment in an employee more likely, and thus the employee gains valuable knowledge and training. The assumed end result is that noncompetes are good for everyone. The problem with this logic, however, is that a growing body of research refutes each level of this claim. Evidence from economics and human psychology suggests that when noncompete agreements are prevalent, stakeholders actually suffer. For regions, employers, and especially employees, noncompete agreements appear to be doing more harm than good.

A strong body of evidence suggests not only that the states and regions that enforce noncompete clauses hinder their own ability to grow economically, but also that these states are pushing talented individuals away. The most famous argument against noncompete clauses is the comparison between Silicon Valley's continuous growth and the slow decline of Route 128 in Boston.

When the computing age dramatically increased the pace of technological innovation, both of these regions were poised to take advantage of the shift.[12] Both were close to established cities with large populations from which to draw talent. Both had strong universities located nearby from which to draw ideas and inventions. In the early days, Route 128 had a slight head start in the race, with more than three times more jobs available than Silicon Valley, but it quickly fell behind. Silicon Valley's local growth rate was soon three times larger than Route 128's.

In looking for an explanation, economists honed in on one key difference: the state of California banned noncompete agreements. Beginning in 1872, California state law has voided any type of contract that would restrict an individual from engaging in lawful trade. The California judiciary has consistently held that a noncompete agreement is a violation of an individual's right to choose his or her work.[13]

In 1994, the economic geographer AnnaLee Saxenian completed an exhaustive study of the two regions and offered several observations as to why Silicon Valley overtook Route 128.[14] Saxenian noted that companies in Massachusetts were more formal, more hierarchical, and more vertically integrated (designing and manufacturing their products); likewise, employees seldom rotated through the company or to other companies. Instead, the goal was to simply climb the corporate ladder.

In Silicon Valley, by contrast, companies operated more openly, less formally, and with a much flatter organizational design. Moreover, employees in the Valley moved around a lot, both on new projects and to whole new companies. This pattern created a vast network connecting talented minds and facilitated a rich transfer of ideas with every transfer of employment. Although she never discussed legal factors, Saxenian noted that much of the Silicon Valley culture seemed to correlate with the employment mobility (and thus we can assume by extension the ban on noncompetes) in California.

But what about causation?

That question would be answered by a different group of economists looking at a different state. From 1905 to 1985, the state of Michigan prohibited any contract that would limit individuals from employment — a ban on noncompete agreements.[15] However, in 1985 the state passed a new law that voided that ban. The Michigan Antitrust Reform Act (MARA) repealed dozens of laws, including the original 1905 ban on noncompete agreements. To employers the passing of MARA looked like an opportunity to reintroduce noncompetes; to three professors it looked like an opportunity for research.

The researchers, Matt Marx of MIT, Jasjit Singh of INSEAD, and Lee Fleming of Harvard Business School, decided to examine the effect of MARA. "This is the ideal natural experiment where you take a population of people — namely, the inventors in Michigan before the law changed — and then you subject them to this shift in enforcement," explained Fleming.[16] Using the US patent database, the researchers tracked the emigration of inventors away from Michigan and compared the state's emigration rate to the rates in states that did not enforce noncompetes. They found that after MARA passed, the rate of inventors fleeing Michigan increased while the rate of inventors fleeing states without non-compete enforcement decreased.[17] In other words, inventors left Michigan much more quickly after the state began enforcing limits on their mobility, and they were moving to states that didn't have noncompetes. These results strongly imply that, by enforcing noncompete agreements, states create a real brain drain as their most talented knowledge workers depart.

But what about those companies that do enforce noncompete agreements? After all, even if it's not good for the region, perhaps it is still good for the company?

Again, the research makes a different case. Researchers from the University of Maryland and the Wharton School found that when an employee switches from one firm to another, both firms may actually benefit.[18] Rafael Corredoira and Lori Rosenkopf studied semiconductor companies for almost fifteen years, from 1980 until 1994, and the patents that those firms filed with the US Patent and Trademark Office. In total, the pair studied 154 firms and 42,000 patents.

In particular, they were interested in the linkages formed between companies when talent departed, as represented in the filing of patents. For every patent application filed, the applicant must cite existing patents from which the new idea borrows or on which it builds. Thus, if employees move from one firm to another, the researchers assumed, they would be able to see the effect of their ideas on the new firm because those employees would be likely to cite patents from their old firm in their new patent applications. This is, after all, the main argument for noncompete clauses in the first place: *to prevent departing employees from taking ideas owned by the old firm with them.*

But surprisingly, the researchers found that when employees leave a firm, both the old and the new firm begin citing each other's patents more often. This suggests that when an employee leaves for another firm, the old company still gains knowledge. The researchers theorized that this happens because of the network linkage created by departing employees. When employees leave an organization, they take ideas as well as relationships with them to the new firm, and their former coworkers left behind in the old firm gain a connection to the new firm and the ex-employee's new ideas. In effect, departing employees have a cross-pollinating effect on the ideas of both organizations.

Surprisingly, this effect was even more significant when the two firms were located far away from each other. The implication is that, given the distance, the old firm would never have encountered the ideas of the new firm without the departing employee moving between them. These findings seem counterintuitive, given the original logic of the noncompete agreement, but the evidence is strong. Companies that rigidly enforce a noncompete clause might actually be suffering, either because their employees aren't leaving (and hence losing the opportunity to create new bridges to unknown ideas) or because departing employees are having to enter whole new industries (where the new bridges are to ideas that are significantly less useful to the old firm). In short, when employees lose freedom of mobility, employees lose their access to intellectual capital.

Beyond the positive effect of departing employees on building a wealth of new ideas, noncompete agreements might be draining value from organizations simply because of the employees who stay. Research suggests that when employees have to work under the restriction of noncompete agreements, they become less motivated and less productive.[19]

Two scholars at the University of San Diego, On Amir and Orly Lobel, studied the effect of noncompetes on individuals inside a simulated market environment. The duo recruited 1,028 participants to an online experiment. The participants were assigned randomly to complete one of two types of tasks. The first task involved finding two numbers in a matrix that would add up to exactly 10; participants were told to correctly complete as many matrices as they could in the time allowed.

The other task involved finding a word that would provide a connection between trios of words, commonly called a "remote associates" task. (For example, the words *peach, tar,* and *arm* are all connected by the word *pit: peachpit, tarpit, armpit*). The matrix task was considered an effort-based task; the remote associates task was considered a creativity-based task. Amir and Lobel theorized that, if internal motivation is stronger during tests of creativity, there might be a different effect on participants completing this task.

Once assigned to a task group, participants were told that they would be paid for performance. The more problems they solved, the more money they would make. In addition, if they finished the entire problem set quickly, they would be given a bonus; if they finished correctly and quickly, they would be paid more, but the bonus would still be available if some of the problems were incorrect. All participants were told that if they completed the task, they would be invited to perform another paid task.

Inside each task group, participants were assigned to one of three conditions. The first set of participants were assigned to a noncompete condition: even if they completed their task, they were told, they would be prohibited from working on a similar task for pay. The second set of participants were assigned to a partial noncompete condition: they were put under the same restriction as those in the first condition, but they also had the option of buying out of it by agreeing to give some of their future earnings back to their first "employer" (the first paid task). The final set was a control group, with no restrictions.

Unlike a lot of researchers, Amir and Lobel were interested in measuring more than simply participants' performance on the task — they also wanted to measure their rate of quitting the task. "The strongest economically meaningful behavior stemming from task motivation is foregoing payment by quitting," explained Lobel.[20] A high rate of quitting was a sign that one of the conditions was causing significant demotivation. And quitting was a big factor.

In analyzing the results, Amir and Lobel found that 61 percent of the participants in the pure noncompete condition gave up on their task in the end (foregoing all payment), compared to a 41 percent quitting rate in the control group. In addition, among the participants who did not quit, those in the noncompete conditions were twice as likely to answer items incorrectly; they also skipped over more items and spent less time overall on the task.

All of these findings suggest that subjecting individuals to noncompete conditions significantly lowers their motivation. Low motivation not only triggers a decrease in their productivity but also increases the likelihood that they will make more mistakes. The implication is striking: noncompete agreements may keep performers inside an organization, but they may also keep people from becoming performers.

Non-noncompete Environments

Between the positive effect of mobility on individual employees' motivation and productivity and the positive increases to intellectual capital for firms even when employees depart, the current body of evidence favors companies and leaders who offer more freedom to their people. Some companies haven't waited for all the evidence — they found out long ago that doing the opposite of noncompete has helped their organization immensely. They benefit from creating *non*-noncompete environments — cultures where ideas are openly shared even with people outside of the organization.

Wieden+Kennedy (W+K), for example, has always been known for resisting the traditions of the Madison Avenue advertising firms it competes against. W+K was founded out of the partnership of Dan Wieden and David Kennedy on April Fool's Day in 1982.[21] Since then, it has grown from its roots in a basement apartment in Portland, Oregon, to become one of the largest independent advertising agencies in the world. Along the way, it has developed a reputation for irreverence and excellence in its work on campaigns such as Coca-Cola, Proctor & Gamble, and Nike. Wieden is actually credited as the creator of Nike's famous "Just Do It" slogan.

Since 2004, one of the programs fueling W+K's success is "WK12," an in-house advertising school. Each year, WK12 accepts a new class of about a dozen students to learn the W+K way of advertising and develop their own portfolios. Applicants typically don't come from traditional marketing programs at business schools, and most of them have almost no advertising experience. In true W+K fashion, the original application for the program was a 5"×8" envelope and instructions to fill it out with whatever applicants thought would get them accepted. Once accepted, they pay tuition to W+K and cover their own living expenses as they study. Although formal classes are often offered during the day, there isn't really a set schedule of classes, as in a typical school. Instead, students rotate in and out of working on real projects for real clients. The students also work on structured assignments, internal company problems, and self-initiated projects.

The program is not an internship, however, as a job at W+K isn't guaranteed, or even likely. "It was always made clear that any expectation of being hired at the end was misplaced," said Jelly Helm, who founded and ran the program for several years.[22] Instead, it's intended to give W+K a constant injection of new ideas and fresh perspectives. Because it's not a job, WK12 can't exactly enforce a noncompete. But it's likely that W+K wouldn't try anyway. Instead, WK12 is a deal made between outside voices and the company itself. The firm provides a unique opportunity to learn from it and to build a portfolio, and WK12 provides insightful ideas and solutions that W+K wouldn't otherwise develop. When both parties go their separate ways (and many graduates are indeed hired by competitors), everyone is better off because of the exchange. As an experiment, WK12's non-noncompete environment has created a petri dish for amazing ideas. While WK12 is currently on hiatus, the expectation is that it will continue to evolve and continue to bring amazing ideas from transient influences.

The idea of bringing individuals into a non-noncompete environment to learn and develop as they work on real company projects isn't new; it's been going on in science and engineering for a long time. In the 1980s, IBM began a postdoctoral program at Almaden Lab in San Jose, California.[23] The lab hired newly minted PhDs (mostly from Stanford University just down the street) in an arrangement similar to a postdoctoral fellowship at a research university. The new postdocs would work for IBM for one to two years and assist with IBM's projects while learning more about their field. Then they would move on either to a faculty position at a university or to another organization.

In this postdoctoral fellowship situation, a non-noncompete environment emerged (no doubt heightened by the decision to locate the lab in California, where a noncompete would be unenforceable anyway). IBM's leaders knew that they would lose talent, but trusted that IBM would benefit from allowing that talent to bring in new ideas and then depart to connect IBM with other institutions down the road. Those connections would lead to new ideas, just as Corredoira and Rosenkopf showed in their study of the semiconductor industry.

In fact, in a study of inventor networks in Silicon Valley, researchers Lee Fleming and Koen Frenken found that the Almaden Lab was a major hub in the larger interorganizational network of the Valley.[24] That network would also strengthen IBM's reputation and image in the industry and allow it to recruit even more new talent. The reputation and network of connections built up by the Almaden Lab certainly helped IBM pivot its business model and stay afloat as the industry moved away from mainframe computers.

When the dot-com bubble burst in the 1990s, IBM's postdoctoral fellowship went into hibernation. It was awakened recently, however, and has now been emulated by several other major companies in the Silicon Valley area.[25] Google, Microsoft, Yahoo!, Intel, and Hewlett-Packard all staff high-quality research centers with postdoctoral fellows, and yet few of these fellows are expected to make the company that hired them their permanent home.

A new program developed by Proctor & Gamble takes the idea of the non-noncompete environment to another level of commitment. For many decades, P&G was noted for its culture of secrecy, including even strict rules for conversations about company products and programs outside of the workplace and rules against conversations with employees of competitors.[26] Not surprisingly, that level of secrecy led to stagnation in the P&G product line and a decline in innovation.

By 2000, the effect of that decline had even affected the company's financials as the company saw its stock price more than cut in half. In 2000 the company leadership fell to A.G. Lafley, a longtime P&G executive. His vision for turning the company around involved also turning the culture of secrecy around. Lafley believed that, to stay competitive, the company had to recognize that it needed its competitors. He calculated that, instead of P&G's 7,500-person research and development operation, there were potentially over one million people whose knowledge the company needed to tap into. So "Research and Development" became "Connect + Develop."

The goal of Connect + Develop was to have over 50 percent of Proctor & Gamble's innovation coming from ideas generated or developed outside of the company.[27] To achieve this, P&G needed to replace its silos and walls with networks. The company created several lines of communication with academic researchers, suppliers, and sometimes even competitors dedicated to finding and cross-pollinating ideas. The goal was to work on ideas that could meet the needs of consumers, whether or not the idea came from in-house, and develop those ideas adjacent to an existing P&G brand. For example, P&G partnered with the Italian chemical company Zobele to build up its Febreze brand by launching several new air-freshening products under the Febreze name.[28] The partnership would be credited with turning Febreze into a $1 billion brand name, and it wouldn't have been possible without partnering with an Italian chemical company that, under the old mentality, would have been a competitor.

Connect + Develop has worked so well that the company launched its own online portal where anyone could submit ideas. Instead of forbidding conversations with competitors, the company is now committed to partnering with anyone, from research labs and academia to competitors large and small. This turnaround in mind-set was accompanied by a financial turnaround as well. Since launching Connect + Develop, P&G has more than climbed back from its decline in valuation, much of which has been due to hitting Lafley's target: more than 50 percent of P&G product initiates now rely on collaboration outside of the company.[29]

Although some of the companies discussed in this chapter may still enforce noncompete clauses among select employees, all of them have benefited from developing an environment for their employees in which they can openly share information, even when they're no longer employees. The experiences of these companies provide an encouraging example of current research in practice. Despite the apparent ubiquity of noncompete clauses everywhere from churches to sandwich shops, evidence from economics and psychology suggests that the benefits of noncompetes usually fail to outweigh the costs on the people who sign them and on the companies that promote them. Greater benefits, in fact, come from giving talent and information real freedom and building non-noncompete environments.

7

■

DITCH PERFORMANCE APPRAISALS

Performance appraisals have long been assumed to be vitally important to a manager's job. But many companies have found that rigid performance management structures actually prevent people from improving their performance, so smart leaders have begun eliminating these structures in favor of newer measures that actually enhance performance.

UNTIL 2012, the performance management process at Adobe Systems worked pretty much as it did at any other large company. Once a year, Adobe's more than 11,000 employees and managers would meet to conduct the annual performance evaluation — the axis on which most performance management systems revolve. That all changed in early 2012, however, when a jet-lagged executive unwittingly started down a path that would end up leaving Adobe's annual review in the dust.[1]

In March 2012, Donna Morris, then senior vice president of human resources at Adobe, had just arrived in India to spend time at Adobe's offices there when she agreed to an interview with a reporter from India's *Economic Times*. During the interview, Morris was asked what she could do to disrupt HR.

Sleep-deprived from the long flight, Morris answered back quickly, "We plan to abolish the annual performance review format."[2] Although she had already been pondering this idea — and had even assembled a small team to discuss it — Morris had yet to discuss anything with Adobe's CEO. Indeed, the company wasn't making any official plans to revise its system.

However, the reporter ran with the quote, and the next day Morris's comments were public record on the front page in an article headlined "Adobe Systems Set to Scrap Annual Appraisals, to Rely on Regular Feedback to Reward Staff." In an effort to get ahead of the story, Morris engaged the communications team at Adobe, and within a few days of her return to the United States she published an article on the company intranet calling on everyone to engage in an assessment of Adobe's current methods for evaluating performance. Ironically, the article quickly became the most-read piece on the company's intranet and generated an overwhelming amount of discussion and momentum for real change with performance appraisals.

Before Morris's fateful trip to India, Adobe's annual review was pretty standard. Once a year, managers would collect examples of past performance, conduct 360-degree evaluations for each employee, and draw up a report on each employee's performance for the year. Then the manager would assign an overall rating to each employee from four categories: high performer, strong performer, solid performer, or low performer.

These ratings followed what is often called a "stack ranking" system: employee ratings had to fit into a fixed ranking distribution. "High performer," for example, could be assigned to no more than 15 percent of a manager's team. Doing these rankings properly was in many ways a costly process. Adobe estimated that a total of 80,000 hours of its managers' time was required each year to conduct all of the reviews, the equivalent of nearly forty full-time employees working year-round. In addition, Adobe saw a spike in voluntary attrition every year in the months following the review, which could only be attributed to disappointed employees deciding to leave after receiving ratings below their expectations.

Reasons such as these added fuel to the fire of discussion that Morris called for in her intranet article. Stating her thesis, Morris wrote that, "ultimately, we need to accomplish three things: review contributions, reward accomplishments, and give and receive feedback. Do they need to be conflated into a cumbersome process? I don't think so. It's time to think radically differently."[3]

Morris called on employees across Adobe to help her craft a new and better way. "If we did away with our 'annual review,' what would you like to see in its place? What would it look like to inspire, motivate, and value contributions more effectively?"

The timing of Morris's call to change Adobe's performance model perfectly mirrored a change going on in the company's overall business model.[4] At the time, Adobe was a thirty-year-old company that had established itself as a premier source of software for creative industry professionals. Like many software companies founded around that time, it had a business model that involved distributing its products through retail stores that would sell boxed installation discs and license codes. Once a year (or whenever necessary), Adobe would use the same channels to release an updated version of the software that improved features and fixed technical glitches. These updated versions also brought new license sales for the company. After three decades of this model, however, technology had been developed that allowed Adobe to distribute its software entirely through the Internet. In

2011 Adobe began changing its business model to a cloud-based subscription model. Users could download Adobe software online and sign up to pay a recurring monthly fee for the software they needed to access.

The company was moving away from its three-decade-old business model, but had left in place performance management systems that were just about as old. If Adobe's customers wanted more real-time engagement, why wouldn't their employees benefit from a similar process? As Morris began interacting with employees and collecting feedback about the current process, one thing became clear: the annual performance review was getting a failing grade. So Morris and Adobe made good on their promise in the *Economic Times* and abolished the annual performance evaluation.

By the fall of 2012, Adobe had totally redesigned its performance management system to eliminate the yearly performance review session and replace it with a more frequent and less formal "check-in" process. The check-in approach was the real-time solution that Morris and Adobe employees were looking for. Managers and employees meet for check-in discussions at least once a quarter (although many schedule check-ins every month or after a project is completed). The discussion isn't scripted, and no paperwork is filled out. However, every check-in discussion centers around three topics: expectations, feedback, and growth and development.

The discussion of expectations involves setting, tracking, and reviewing clear objectives for the individual's job and current projects. During this talk, roles and responsibilities are clarified, as well as measurements of success. Expectations flow from senior leadership's presentation of company goals on what remains an annual basis, but managers and employees collaboratively discuss how employees' positions and complete projects help fulfill those goals. The expectations are recorded so that they can inform future check-in sessions.

As Morris realized, employees wanted feedback on their projects that was more frequent and timely. They also wanted coaching from managers on their recent performance compared to the expectations to show where they were and whether the expectations needed to be adjusted upward or downward. Now that feedback is included in the regular check-ins, employees also have a chance to give managers feedback on how well they are meeting employee' needs.

Including employees' growth and development in the check-ins allows managers and employees to talk about opportunities. Employees examine their current role and their desired career path and then receive advice from managers on the knowledge, skills, and abilities they need to improve in their current role and to move closer to the future they envision for themselves. In contrast to the rearview-mirror perspective provided by most annual reviews, discussing employees' growth and development allows managers and employees to brainstorm on employees' goals and how they align with Adobe's strategy. Most of all, this part of the check-in helps employees own their career and development plan and feel more empowered to grow.

While these three elements became part of much more frequent conversations between employees and managers, some things needed to stay on a yearly schedule. Expectations tended to be set yearly (but could be revised every check-in if needed) to align with the company planning cycle. In addition, compensation decisions were still made only once a year. However, without the "high performer" to "low performer" ratings to gauge merit increases, Adobe shifted ownership of salary decisions to individual managers. Managers were given a set budget and discretion over how to allocate it to their people based on how employees met their expectations.

Changing from the old system to a more frequent, less formal process was a big transition, and so Morris and her team needed to make sure that everyone knew what was changing and why. Adobe hosted sessions to help make employees and managers aware of the change. They also created training sessions for managers to learn how best to structure their check-in sessions. Amazingly, 90 percent of Adobe's managers participated in the training. The company also created an employee resource center to answer frequently asked questions about performance management, career coaching, and making the most of check-ins.

Two years after the death of the old annual review, the check-in process is working brilliantly. Morris has found that morale among employees and managers has increased significantly, largely owing to the more frequent feedback. "The check-ins are a 180[-degree turn] in terms of giving people the material they need to improve their performance and change course," Morris said. "It completely changes how employees feel about their jobs and opportunities. Feedback is now viewed as a gift."

The improvement in morale has led to improvement in hard numbers as well. Adobe has seen a 30 percent decrease in the number of employees quitting and a 50 percent increase in involuntary departures — people who weren't meeting expectations are now dealt with more directly and quickly instead of being able to hide until the next performance cycle. Most importantly, the company has gotten back most of the 80,000 hours spent by managers annually on annual reviews. The success of the performance management shift mirrors Adobe's overall success in its business model shift. In 2014, Adobe's revenue from subscription services surpassed its revenue from packaged licenses, and that revenue continues to rise.

Why Performance Reviews
Get a Failing Grade

As a tool, performance management dates back to the 1930s.[5] While measuring performance dates back a little further — to Frederick Winslow Taylor and his history-making stopwatch — it was Elton Mayo who soon became a rival of Taylor's ideas and provided the spark for the performance management fire. In the famous Hawthorne Works study of workers at the Western Electric Company, Mayo noticed that productivity and morale were directly correlated to how employees felt about the social structure of the organization and whether individuals felt that their manager had an interest in their well-being and success.[6]

Mayo's findings birthed the human relations movement and shifted the role of managers from measuring and enforcing performance standards to coaching people on how to better meet those standards. It didn't take long for these informal acts of coaching to turn into formal meetings. About twenty years after Mayo's insightful research, performance review meetings had become fully embedded in the workplace with the passage of the Performance Rating Act of 1950. The law mandated that all federal employees receive an annual performance evaluation and that their performance be given one of three ratings: outstanding, satisfactory, or unsatisfactory.[7] It wasn't long before these ratings would be connected to bonuses, salary increases, and promotion opportunities.

The critical moment for performance reviews came in the 1980s, when Jack Welch popularized the idea that fixed ratings should also be tied to a forced distribution — that employees should be graded on a curve. As CEO of General Electric, Welch implemented a forced ranking system (also known as "stack ranking" or "rank and yank") that ranks all executives along a three-category bell curve.[8] The A players (the top 20 percent) receive lavish rewards, the B players (the middle 70 percent) get minimal investment, and the C players (the bottom 10 percent) are given a limited window to improve before being shown the door.

Welch's endorsement of the demanding rank-and-yank system led many senior leaders to follow suit, especially since GE experienced nearly a twenty-eight-fold increase in earnings during Welch's twenty-year tenure.[9] Soon a multibillion-dollar industry developed to serve the forced ranking desires of corporate leaders. In 2012, the majority of Fortune 500 companies reported using a performance evaluation system similar to Welch's curve.[10] But the popularity of the now-traditional method has grown alongside widespread disillusionment with performance management. A 2013 survey found that 95 percent of managers were dissatisfied with their performance evaluation process and 90 percent of those who worked in human resources didn't think that performance evaluations were accurate, much less effective at improving productivity.

Bob Sutton, an organizational psychologist at Stanford University, summarized the angst and effectiveness of performance reviews perfectly by comparing them to prescription medication. "If performance evaluations were a drug, they would not receive FDA approval," he told the *New York Times,* because "they have so many side effects, and so often they fail."[11] Speculation about why the annual review is such an ineffective treatment for performance enhancement is wide-ranging and complicated by the intent of the performance review process: to provide feedback that improves performance. Theoretically, following a performance review, employees should be better able to identify growth opportunities and improve their performance. However, that theory is being challenged by more recent research.

To begin with, individuals have differing mind-sets about performance and their confidence that they can even improve. People generally hold one of three perspectives on their own ability to improve and pursue goals. People with a "learning goal orientation" view their performance as flexible and hence capable of improvement with time and effort. People with a "performance-prove goal orientation" are focused on demonstrating their competence but don't necessarily think they can improve. Likewise, people with a "performance-avoidance goal orientation" also view their ability as fixed but try to avoid situations that invite judgment of their performance.[12] Carol Dweck, a psychologist at Stanford University, later popularized a reconception of these three perspectives as two "mind-sets" surrounding growth and achievement: a growth mind-set and a fixed mind-set, with the latter representing both types of performance orientations.[13] Dweck's research found dramatic differences between the two mind-sets when it came to performance improvement in a variety of fields, from learning in primary school to performing in the workplace. Dweck also argued that mind-sets are changeable and can even be primed — that is, that organizations can help their people adopt a growth mind-set and perform even better.

Performance evaluations are perceived differently by individuals depending on their mind-set, but it seemed logical that the performance evaluation could help shape an individual's mind-set. To people with a learning goal orientation, evaluations could be welcomed as a chance to receive the feedback they need to improve. To people with a performance goal orientation, or fixed mind-set, the performance review could either confirm or challenge their perception of their own performance. That being said, the hope was that the performance review could be seen as a chance to adopt a learning goal orientation, or growth mind-set. After all, the common maxim is that it's performance, not the individual, being rated, and that the point of the review is to help the individual achieve higher performance.

That logic, however, didn't appear to hold up when tested. Three researchers, led by Satoris Culbertson, assistant professor of management at Kansas State University, designed a study to test whether goal orientation affects individuals' reactions to performance appraisals and how they process the feedback — in other words, do performance appraisals help them improve their performance or not?[14] Culbertson and her colleagues surveyed 234 staff employees at an undisclosed university in the southwestern United States. The employees had just received a performance evaluation three months prior to the survey. These evaluations included an overall rating that ranged from 1 ("does not meet expectations") to 4 ("outstanding performance"). The researchers asked the staffers to disclose their performance rating, but also to rate their satisfaction with the performance review they had just received, including how happy they were with the feedback they received. In addition, the staffers were asked a series of questions to determine their goal orientation (learning, performance-prove, performance-avoid). Culbertson and her team assumed that those with performance orientations (and thus probably fixed mind-sets) would be dissatisfied with their review, and that those with a learning orientation would have appreciated and used the feedback from the rating. But that isn't what they found.

When they analyzed the results of the survey, they found that those who viewed their rating as negative were disappointed with the evaluation process *regardless* of their goal orientation or mind-set. Performance-oriented employees were dissatisfied, but even those individuals with learning orientations were unhappy with a review meant to help them improve and develop. These results challenged the logic of performance reviews and surprised the researchers. "We thought if anything they'd be able to take it and apply it to their own jobs," Culbertson explains. "But they simply don't like negative feedback, either."[15]

It's important to note that the research team didn't have access to the actual reviews; instead, they were asking employees to self-disclose. In doing so, they captured the employees' *perspectives* on whether the rating was positive or negative, not the manager's intent. This is an important distinction because it emphasizes that what an organization views as a positive review may be viewed quite differently by the employee. In other words, a manager might consider a rating of 3 a positive review, but an employee expecting a 4 would not see it that way.

The researchers' results suggest that even learning-oriented employees, who should be most able to improve, are put off when they receive a rating that is less than expected. This effect is compounded when companies insist that ratings align with a forced ranking or bell curve — a system that intentionally suppresses the number of employees receiving the top rating and hence increases the potential number of disaffected employees. The study's results suggest that nearly everyone, even those who genuinely want to improve, would give their performance evaluation process a low rating.

Improving Performance Without Rating Performance

As evaluations of annual reviews continue to produce a failing grade, more and more companies have begun overhauling their process. Some have abandoned annual performance appraisals entirely, like Donna Morris and Adobe. Others have modified their system to shift away from ratings and reviews and focus instead on discussions that actually increase performance.

In 2013, the software giant Microsoft announced that it was overhauling its performance management process to eliminate many of the problem elements. In a memo to all employees, Microsoft human resources chief Lisa Brummel made it clear what they were moving away from: there would be "no more curve" and "no more ratings."[16] Before the change, Microsoft had developed a reputation for its slow response to market trends, its lack of innovation, and the decline of its value over time. From 2000 to 2012, Microsoft's market capitalization had declined from $510 billion — which made it the largest company in the world — to half of that value.[17]

In an exposé published in *Vanity Fair*, Microsoft employees and executives were unanimous in pointing their finger to one big reason: stack ranking. Stack ranking created a culture where innovative ideas were killed quickly, and anything that might challenge the status quo and hence an employee's rating was hidden. Microsoft's system mirrored the one first promoted by Jack Welch: employees on a team of ten would know at the beginning of the year that only two would be getting a great review and that one of them might be getting shown the door.

As a result, *team members were competing with each other rather than collaborating.* Executives at Microsoft noticed that top performers sought to distance themselves from each other, since having more than two superstars on a team meant that some were going to lose their shine. In addition to inhibiting Microsoft's ability to innovate by pushing top talent away from each other, stack ranking also pushed many top performers out the door to companies where they could just focus on work rather than on making sure their job was safe. Microsoft's new system features more frequent meetings (called "Connects") between managers and employees to provide feedback and a greater emphasis on teamwork and collaboration. Managers and employees also discuss employees' future growth and development during these meetings. "This will let us focus on what matters," Brummel wrote in the memo. "Having a deeper understanding of the impact we've made and our opportunities to grow and improve."[18]

In 2010, Lear Corporation, a Fortune 500 company that supplies the automotive industry, decided to replace annual reviews with quarterly feedback discussions between managers and employees.[19] The company decided that its previous system, which annually evaluated 115,000 employees in thirty-six countries and used those evaluations to determine bonuses and raises, wasn't improving performance. Tom DiDonato, the chief human resources officer at Lear, and his team found that during reviews, honest feedback discussion was being pushed aside by too many people focusing simply on their rating and their raise. The new discussions under the quarterly system have no connection to pay decisions, and to underscore this point Lear has dropped annual individual raises and moved instead to an annual bonus based on company performance. "The way to drive high performance is through honest feedback that employees and managers *really* hear," DiDonato wrote for *Harvard Business Review*. "We've found that our new system greatly improves the feedback process."

In 2012, shortly after Motorola spun off its mobile phone unit, the company also spun off its employee rating system. Like Adobe, Motorola encourages managers and employees to have ongoing feedback sessions in the form of informal conversations about performance. The company still maintains an annual review, though the intent is that nothing discussed should come as a surprise since the annual review is meant to summarize the year's previous discussions.

Most drastically, however, Motorola moved away from its label-based rating system and forced ranking. Before the change, employees were rated with terms like "outstanding performer" or "valued performer," along with a forced ranking, and their ratings were tied to their bonus eligibility. "People had an unbelievable focus on their rating," CEO Greg Brown said in an interview shortly after Motorola made the change. "So we decided to forget the rating and just link pay to performance more directly. You no longer have a forced bell curve, which can be demoralizing and create a culture of infighting."[20] In place of the bell curve, Motorola created a bonus structure with standard payouts based on the company's financial results. Motorola estimates that more frequent conversations still reduced the time spent on reviews by 50 to 70 percent, time that the company has reallocated to finding and developing the right talent.

The travel powerhouse Expedia, Inc., left behind its employee ratings and rankings system in 2010. The parent company of hotels.com, hotwire.com, and (of course), expedia.com found that the once-a-year event was dehumanizing the relationship between managers and employees. Connie Symes, the executive vice president for human resources at Expedia, Inc., explained the organization's rationale: "Over time, the rating system has become this huge obstacle. The employees would see their rating first and then the whole review evolved into a discussion of 'Why this?' 'Why not that?' as opposed to an opportunity to provide meaningful feedback."[21]

After explaining the need through companywide town halls, Expedia's senior leadership team mandated that in lieu of one annual review, managers and employees would now be required to hold one-on-one informal discussions focusing on feedback, performance improvement, and career planning. Moreover, surveys would be sent to the employees asking them to give feedback to managers about the frequency and quality of these conversations. Symes has found that the majority of employees prefer these discussions to rating and ranking events, and that morale improvement has likely helped Expedia expand its travel empire.

Companies that have ditched performance appraisals altogether in favor of methods that focus on performance improvement, like Adobe and Lear, are in the minority. But companies dissatisfied with their current system seem to remain in the majority. For a lot of leaders, the annual review and the concept of performance management go hand in glove. As Microsoft, Motorola, and Expedia have shown, however, it's possible to stay focused on performance without pesky rating or ranking systems. Taken together, the experiences of all of these companies suggest that the best way to improve performance is to build a system that meets the unique needs of the specific organization and its people. For most companies, that begins by giving the performance evaluation itself a thorough performance review. Keep the parts that employees and managers rate as useful, and as for the parts of the process that aren't making the grade — it may be time to show them the door.

8

■

HIRE AS A TEAM

Most managers hire by screening résumés and conducting a few interviews with individual candidates. Later, many of those managers find that a significant percentage of the new hires don't perform as well as they interviewed. To help them make smarter hiring decisions, the best leaders now bring their whole team into the interview process.

EMPLOYEES AT WHOLE FOODS MARKET are called "team members," which is neither a corporate euphemism nor a meaningless cliché. Teams and team members — not positions or stores or regions — are central to the operational core of Whole Foods and the building blocks of the organization.

Each Whole Foods location is built around eight to ten teams, grouped from departments like produce, meat, prepared foods, and checkout. The teams have a remarkable degree of autonomy, helping to decide what to order, how to price items, and how to run promotions. Even outside the store, a team focus continues up the chain of command all the way to the top. Store leaders in the region are considered a team. Even the regional presidents form a team. Founder John Mackey is part of a team — he shares the co-CEO label, and a third person serves as chairman of the board. (Whole Foods is a publicly traded company.)

The company even calls its mission statement a "Declaration of Interdependence," claiming that Whole Foods is first and foremost a community of people working together to create value for other people.[1] The team focus is so strong that Whole Foods even allows teams to select who gets to join their team.

Whole Foods started as a single location in 1980, though this location was birthed out of the merger of two smaller health and natural foods stores.[2] John Mackey, who two years earlier had started a small natural foods store called Saferway (a pun on the local supermarket, Safeway), joined forces with another store to form the new store. At 10,500 square feet with a staff of nineteen people, Whole Foods Market was a natural foods store that looked like a small supermarket, but it retained the culture of the hometown natural foods store. The hope was that its size and offerings could provide a full-service, natural-foods option to more traditional grocery shoppers.

Over the past thirty-five years, shoppers appear to have really appreciated this option. Today Whole Foods Market has more than 400 stores in three countries and employs nearly 60,000 people. The company went public in 1992, and since then the stock price has increased over 3,000 percent. As it expanded, keeping the original culture intact became a chief concern, especially since much of the company's growth was fueled by mergers and acquisitions. Designing around semi-autonomous teams became one way to reinforce that culture. Hiring new members through a team effort was another — and perhaps even more effective — way to ensure that the DNA of the Whole Foods culture continued to replicate. As a result, the company's dramatic growth has occurred alongside its perennial appearance on *Fortune*'s "100 Best Companies to Work For" every year since the list began.[3]

The hiring process for new team members is unconventional for a supermarket. Like the design of the company, it runs on team input. New associates undergo a sixty-day process that involves a variety of interviews. There are phone interviews, one-to-one interviews with store leaders, and panel interviews with teams built from recruiters, managers, and select employees. When new associates come on board, the store leader places them on a team, but only provisionally. After the trial period, the existing team votes on whether to fully vest the new associate into their team. It takes a two-thirds majority vote from the team to become an employee. The voting step is required, but how the vote is taken is left up to the team. New associates who don't get a two-thirds vote are off the team and must either find a new team to join — and repeat the trial period — or just leave the company.[4] This team selection process happens for every new member, from cashiers on checkout teams to financial analysts in the home office.

The rationale behind such a team-focused process is that bringing new people into the company is a critical decision and critical decisions should be made by the people most affected by their outcomes. In this case, deciding who to bring onto a team is best made by the team itself. In addition, being given the authority to welcome or to veto a new team member helps everyone on the team take ownership of their performance. Since the majority of new hires are welcomed onto the team, rejecting a hire is an important moment for the existing team. Until they've stood up to a leader and said, "This person isn't a good fit for us; go back and try again," they haven't truly declared their interdependence. "A team doesn't fully gel until it doesn't vote somebody on the team," said John Mackey.[5]

Ensuring that new hires are a good fit for individual teams is also vital because teams are the basic unit of measurement for performance.[6] Whole Foods makes performance data for every team in every store widely available across the entire company. Teams are given their profit per labor-hour every four weeks, as well as their historical performance, the performance of other teams in their store, and the performance of similar teams in other stores. Teams compete against similar teams and also against themselves to continue to improve performance.

In fact, the company shares so much performance data with its team members that the Securities and Exchange Commission has designated every team member an "insider" when it comes to stock trading. This makes incentives tricky, especially since stock options are distributed as widely as performance data. Over 90 percent of stock options have been given to non-executives. By contrast, in most of the other Fortune 500 companies, more than 75 percent of stock options are granted to fewer than six senior executives.

Bonuses are even paid out based on team data. The company calls it "gainsharing"—that is, the higher a team's performance gains, the more the team members gain in bonus pay. So it's important for team members to consider how an individual will affect the quality of their team, especially low-performing individuals who manage to convince a hiring manager that they are star performers. "You can always fool the team leader, but it's very hard to fool the team," Mackey explained. "The team can see through you." The aim of the Whole Foods method of hiring as a team is to underscore the importance of teams and to address the dilemma of how to avoid hiring people who appear to be great performers but don't actually perform as well as represented. The method is especially brilliant in light of recent research suggesting the importance of teams in producing great performers.

Why Hiring Is a Team Affair

Traditionally, we have tended to believe that job performance is solely an individual matter, determined by the abilities and motivation of the individual employee. Many organizations and leaders act as if talent and abilities are fully portable from one organization to another. We have built management systems fully based on the premise of training, motivating, and rewarding individuals for their performance. This long-held belief only got stronger with the shift from industrial age work to knowledge work. Even the legendary management guru Peter Drucker advocated for this perspective, writing that "knowledge workers, unlike manual workers in manufacturing, own the means of production: they carry that knowledge in their heads and can therefore take it with them."[7]

But research on the causes of performance and its portability is building toward an alternative perspective. Several recent studies suggest that a significant part, if not the majority, of individual performance is better attributed to the team or organization to which the performers belong than to the performers themselves. It turns out not to be so easy to separate out individual and team performance. And it's even harder to spot the potential for performance in an individual candidate.

The most significant evidence for this new perspective on what makes for high performance comes not from the grocery store floors of Whole Foods but from the trading floors of Wall Street. Wall Street's industry perspective is almost purely one that rewards individual performance. From salaries and bonuses to hiring practices, performance is almost entirely tied to the sole performer. This perspective made the findings of a team of professors from Harvard Business School particularly surprising. If knowledge workers really do own their means of production, then can they take their level of performance with them to new firms? Is performance portable?

This is the question that these researchers, led by Boris Groysberg, sought to answer.[8] Groysberg and his team collected nine years of data on the performance of Wall Street stock analysts, the people who write the reports about companies and industries that investors, mutual fund advisers, and others use to make investment decisions. Analyzing data and writing reports appears to be a fairly solitary endeavor, and one that ought to rely on purely individual talents. The team collected performance information on star analysts by creating a database out of analysts' rankings in *Institutional Investor,* which annually surveys money managers on which analysts have been the most helpful and then compiles a ranking of first, second, and third, with a runner-up. Groysberg and his team collected rankings data between 1988 and 1996 and built a database of 1,052 analysts ranked over those nine years. They then added information about whether those analysts had moved from one firm to another. To round out their quantitative data, they also surveyed analysts from twenty-four investment banks and conducted 167 hours of interviews.

With these data in hand, the team was able to analyze what happened when star performers switched companies. They found three surprising consequences. The first was that the stars' performance declined. Stars often dropped in the rankings. *Those who jumped saw an average of a 20 percent drop in the first year, and their performance hadn't returned to the old level even after five years.* The second finding was that the performance of the new group declined as well, as the new former star performer disrupted the new group's communication and sometimes created personal conflicts. The third consequence was a decline in the company's overall valuation. Despite the individual perspective on talent, over time hiring individual stars was seen by the market as a negative.

Interestingly, however, they found that one type of acquisition didn't experience the same drops in performance as the rest: lift-outs. A lift-out is the acquisition of the entire team that surrounds an individual. Analysts who switched employers but brought their team with them ended up performing far better than the solo movers. In fact, when teams moved, they suffered no significant decrease in performance at all. To explain this difference, Groysberg and his team suspect that, when individuals change employers, they give up a lot of resources that contributed to their past success. However, if they move with a team, even though they lose their old company's resources, they can at least bring some social resources with them. Being able to bring along those resources apparently helps offset the loss of company resources.

The results of this study suggest that there is more to team performance than the individual performer, but how much of performance is explained by the team? If lift-outs prevent a decline in performance, what is the effect of teams on individual performance?

To answer this, Groysberg returned to his database of investment analysts and their rankings.[9] This time he and his team organized the analysts by their company and teams. The researchers' goal was to determine how many teams and firms featured a collection of star performers (analysts ranked by *Institutional Investor*) and whether having ranked colleagues had an effect on individuals' performance — both where they were ranked in a given year and their chances of improving their ranking the next year.

When they examined the new data set, the researchers found that coworkers were indeed a significant contributor to individual performance. Although the past ranking of star performers was a good predictor of their future ranking, individual analysts were far more likely to stay ranked or improve in rank if they had other star performers on their team or in their firm.

In other words, the more talented the team, the better the individual performance. Groysberg and his team suggest that the quality of colleagues affects individual performance in four main ways: colleagues become sources of useful information, they give insightful feedback, they act as an important connection between the individual analyst and the firm's clients, and they enhance the individual analyst's reputation.[10] The implications of their study are just as simple: if you want to get the best out of individuals, make sure to treat them as members of a team and not as solo performers.

It may seem like a long journey from the trading floors of Wall Street to the grocery stores of Whole Foods, and it's important not to overgeneralize from these studies. However, the research into colleague quality and the impact of lift-outs does help explain the benefits of hiring in teams. Although not every organization can afford to hire whole teams of people at a time, this research suggests that careful consideration can still be given to the individual candidates and the teams they're being considered for. If the candidate and the team are a good fit, then the quality and cohesion of the team will enhance everyone's performance. If not, then it doesn't matter if the candidate was faking talent or really is a star performer. That person isn't likely to be a star for much longer.

In traditional organizations, from organic grocers to white-collar businesses, hiring is often a solo endeavor. Individual candidates are interviewed by individual managers, often in multiple rounds of one-to-one interviews. Sometimes panel interviews are utilized, but more often than not the number of people a candidate interacts with before being offered a position is kept to a minimum. After all, who wants to spend too much time on "nonessentials" like hiring?

When new hires arrive on the team, the team leader or manager may be the only person they have met. When this is the case, it's unlikely that much consideration was paid to person-team fit. By contrast, organizations that hire as a team are better able to assess that fit and make new individual hires seem almost like lift-outs. When a Whole Foods team votes on whether to make a new hire a permanent team member, they are voting on whether or not that person can improve the quality of the team and whether they can improve the performance of that person. That's a big difference.

Different Teams Require Different Team Hiring Methods

Whole Foods started hiring as a team because teams work closely with each other on the store floor. But surprisingly, even companies that work entirely with teams distributed virtually across the globe benefit from a hiring process that allows them to gain experience working closely with their future colleagues. The web development company Automattic does this by holding auditions for new candidates, a step in the hiring process they call "trials."

Founded by Matt Mullenweg, Automattic is the maker of WordPress software, the most popular blogging platform on the Internet. The 450-person company has employees in thirty-seven countries around the world, though it keeps an office in San Francisco that functions like a coworking space.[11] In the early years, Mullenweg hired the traditional way, screening résumés and conducting interviews. While Automattic would sometimes have candidates interact with a panel of current employees, Mullenweg was disappointed every time someone who seemed like a good fit ended up not being one — and sometimes up to one-third of new hires didn't work out.

Mullenweg needed a better way. He concluded that the traditional process allowed too much influence from factors that didn't
really contribute to performance once a candidate was hired.
What mattered was not just how well candidates would work, but
how well they would work with their team. To get a sense of this,
the best thing to do was to get them working. So Mullenweg over-
hauled Automattic's process and made the cornerstone of the new
process the trial.

"Trials as a hiring technique really came from trial-and-error,"
he explained. "We noticed in the early days that some of our best
people were coming from our open source area. They'd built
things that worked with WordPress, and when we hired them,
they did great work."[12] Candidates applying to work at Automattic still have their résumé reviewed by Mullenweg, and they still
receive a fairly traditional initial interview. However, the next step
breaks drastically from tradition. Candidates who seem like a
good match get a chance to try out for their position.

Automattic places them on a real project team and even gives
them all of the security access and permissions they need to work
like an already hired employee. Candidates applying to work in
customer support are put right in front of customers. Engineering
candidates write real code. Designers design. While one person
supervises the candidate during the trial, candidates interact with
more people in the company as it progresses. Because Automattic
is a distributed company and teams work virtually, candidates can
work anywhere and at any time. Most work during their trial for
ten to twenty hours per week, often before or after their current
job. Automattic pays every candidate a standard, and fair-market,
hourly wage.

The trial period can last anywhere from three to eight weeks,
depending on the person and the project. The intent isn't necessarily to have the candidate complete a project. Instead, the trial

period takes as long as is needed for the team to make an accurate assessment of what it's like working with the candidate, and for the candidate to get a feel for Automattic. What candidates work on during tryouts "may not be exactly what the person will be working on once they're hired, but we're looking at a lot of things besides just their work," Mullenweg explained. "Communication is super-important, so we're testing for how well they communicate and how well they handle feedback. We've found that a common trait of high performers is how open they are to feedback."

Mullenweg recognizes that the trial process makes it impossible for some people to apply, but he believes that it's useful as a filter that screens out candidates who aren't serious. "We don't want trials to be a hurdle that just weeds people out," he said, "but hurdles can be good too — if you have a place where people want to work, where people are willing to do what's necessary to succeed, and who are passionate enough about Automattic to make the process a priority."[13]

If a candidate "passes" the trial and the team he or she worked with decides that the candidate would be a good fit, then the final round is an interview with Mullenweg himself. In an effort to strip even that interview of factors that influence interviewers but don't influence performance, Mullenweg does the interview entirely through a text-only online chat. Mullenweg estimates 95 percent of people who pass the trial get a job offer. His goal in the final interview is just to get a sense of the candidate's passion and cultural fit that the team picked up on during the trial.

Once candidates accept an offer, it's time to get a sense for how they interact with Automattic's most important team: their customers. Regardless of the position they applied for, new hires spend their first three weeks working with the customer support team.

The trial and team assessment process appears to be working.

Automattic has grown significantly since instituting the process, and that growth has been fueled by new hires who can perform because they're part of a team. "When we hire someone at Automattic," Mullenweg told the *Harvard Business Review,* "we want the relationship to last for decades."[14] And it looks like Automattic stands a good chance of hitting that milestone. Mullenweg estimates that the company hires only about 40 percent of the people who go through the trial process, but those hires tend to stick around. In 2013 Automattic hired 101 people, and only two of them left the company.

In the history of the company up until 2014, according to Mullenweg, 370 people have been hired and only 60 of them have left.[15] Beyond low turnover, Automattic has also seen high growth. By some estimates, WordPress (the company's main product) powers 22 percent of websites across the entire Internet.[16] In March 2014, Automattic closed a series C round of financing and raised $160 million from investors, valuing the company at $1.16 billion.

Mullenweg believes that auditioning job candidates and letting them interact with a real project team is a big part of Automattic's success. Yes, trials are a big investment of time for the people involved. But they're seen as a worthwhile investment. "It's considered an honor to be put on the hiring group," Mullenweg said. "Everyone in the company recognizes that one of the most important decisions you can make is who to bring on the team."[17]

How Google Works

Trial periods working with their future team may provide a realistic preview of candidates' true performance potential, but they may not be feasible for every company. However, there are other steps that can be taken to redesign the standard hiring process. Another technology company—perhaps the most famous technology company of all—makes sure that new candidates interview not only with their team but with a variety of people who might one day be on their team. That company is Google—famous not just for its products but for its company culture, which starts at hiring.

From the beginning, Google has been trusting teams to make hiring decisions, even back when those team interviews were conducted around the Ping-Pong table that was the company's first conference table. "Larry [Page] and Sergey [Brin] always insisted that hiring decisions be made by groups rather than a single manager," said Laszlo Bock, the senior vice president of people operations at Google.[18] Google's commitment to involving so many people is noteworthy, because Google receives over 2 million applications each year and hires only a few thousand. The company has calculated its acceptance rate and found that Google is more selective than Yale, Princeton, and Harvard.

Google's hiring process involves several steps, starting with an initial résumé screen and remote interview with a recruiter, then proceeding to interviews with the hiring manager, peers, cross-functional managers, and even future subordinates.[19] Being interviewed by the people who will work for you is a very different approach, but one that is also very aligned with Groysberg's research. "In a way," said Bock, "their assessments are more important than anyone else's—after all, they're going to have to live with you."

After that, the feedback from all the interviews is compiled and given to two different committees charged with reviewing each applicant in turn and making an accept or reject decision. These committees typically don't have anyone on the candidate's future team, but everyone could be a teammate in the future. The committees help the teams conducting interviews to stay calibrated to a uniform standard of quality and even serve as a feedback mechanism for interviewers. Lastly, if the committees vote to accept, the application and all notes from the committees are forwarded to CEO Larry Page, who makes the final decision on every new hire.

Google is also committed to using experimentation and data to shape its hiring practice. At one point, interviewing as a team meant that one candidate could have up to twenty-five different interviews with various people. It wasn't until the company studied its recent hires and found that, with only four interviews, they could decide with an 86 percent confidence rate whether or not to hire someone; each additional interview added only 1 percent to the confidence rate. They also found that no one person could gather enough information to make the decision.

Many companies don't have the luxury of time to make hiring decisions this way, but that doesn't mean they can't benefit from utilizing the whole team. One company, Kalama, Washington–based Steelscape, has surrendered its hiring process almost entirely to the teams that potential new hires would be working on.[20] At first glance, the factories at Steelscape, which manufactures steel coils for the construction industry, resemble those first examined by Frederick Winslow Taylor at the turn of the twentieth century, with one important distinction: Steelscape runs on self-directed teams. In fact, during the night shift supervisors aren't even present. Because the company is entirely dependent on how well its teams operate, Steelscape handed its hiring process over to those teams.

The first step for job applicants is taking a pre-employment screening test to assess their skills. Everyone who passes the test is then invited to join a "pre-orientation" session in which they are given information about Steelscape and how the company operates. During this phase, candidates are also called in for an interview, typically with a panel of up to six manufacturing associates (their potential teammates) who have been trained in how to ask the right questions and listen for the right answers.

Human resources representatives are always present at these interviews, but their role is simply to observe; the team is in charge. After interviewing all of the candidates, the associates debrief and assess which candidates would be the best fit. The top four candidates are invited back for a second round of interviews with a new team of associates. If these associates decide that a candidate would be a good fit, an offer is made.

Unlike Whole Foods or Automattic, Steelscape uses what looks like a more traditional hiring method, but with individual interviews turned over to teams. Using this method, they can hire more quickly; the average time from application to offer is just two weeks. Not that quick hiring is needed — Steelscape's turnover rate is an astoundingly low 1.6 percent, and productivity remains high. Steelscape's hiring process even led to its receipt of a "best practices" award from the American Psychological Association's Center for Organizational Effectiveness.

While the hiring processes at Whole Foods, Automattic, Google, and Steelscape all look fairly different, the core philosophy is the same: *the people who work with new hires should be the ones deciding whether or not they're hired.* Behind this simple philosophy is hard evidence that individual performance isn't entirely individual. Gauging a new employee's potential for performance is difficult, and knowing if that person will work up to that potential is even harder — especially when the job falls to a lone manager. The variety of examples and empirical research described in this chapter all yield the same implication — the most accurate way to judge performance potential is to have the judging done by the colleagues who will affect much of that performance.

9

WRITE THE ORG CHART IN PENCIL

Constructing rigid hierarchies and enforcing them through a fixed structure may have worked in older industries like the railroad industry, but the nature of work today demands an organizational chart that can handle change. The best leaders write their organizational chart in pencil, allowing the best teams to form around problems and products, instead of drawing lines and boxes in ink.

E DEN MCCALLUM IS a consulting firm with no consultants and no proprietary methodologies or tools. Founded in 2000, just as the dot-com bubble was bursting, Eden McCallum operates on a wholly different model than the big three (McKinsey, Boston Consulting Group, and Bain).

Traditionally, consulting firms have recruited freshly minted MBAs from elite universities across the globe. These junior consultants are then placed in an office and funneled into client projects that were acquired by the senior partners (who often go "missing in action" shortly after signing up the client). The junior consultants put in grueling hours for several years before moving on to new career opportunities or (hopefully) making partner. Partners themselves spend less and less time on client projects as they move up the organizational chart and more and more time recruiting new clients.

Very few of these elements appear in Eden McCallum's organizational design, and that just might be its strongest competitive advantage.

Eden McCallum was founded by two partners, Liann Eden and Dena McCallum, both of whom were former consultants at McKinsey & Company.[1] They met in 1991 while each was studying for an MBA at INSEAD, but went their separate ways — Eden joined Unilever and moved to London and McCallum became a consultant at McKinsey in her hometown of Toronto. Just four years later, the two were reunited when they started working as consultants for McKinsey's London office. The two were separated again when McCallum joined Condé Nast as the director of strategy and planning. Shortly afterward, Eden also left McKinsey, this time owing to the birth of her first child — and the birth of the duo's new business.

Around the time that the dot-com bubble was reaching its peak, both Eden and McCallum had noticed a growing trend among consultants. Many of the people who left the world of consulting for executive positions found that they missed the culture of professional services, but they sure didn't miss the intense pressure that came with being a part of those firms. Others had jumped ship during the bubble to wade into the waters of entrepreneurship, but were washed ashore when the economy stopped raging.[2] In addition, as many of the former consultant class grew up in the ranks of the companies for which they had once consulted, the need for those organizations to retain the expense of a top-level consulting firm diminished. The companies still needed consultants for certain projects, just not as often and not a small army of consultants.

"It was this coming together of clients who said: 'I really want a different way of working and engaging with strategy issues,'" Liann Eden explained. "And then a group of current and former consultants saying, 'I really want a different way of working, because I have some issues with the traditional consulting firm.'"[3] Eden and McCallum knew there was potential for an alternative to consulting as usual.

That alternative took the form of a new kind of organizational chart—one built without organizational lines, boxes, or hierarchy. Instead, it was built around the concept of a network and split the traditional consulting partner role into two roles: client development and project delivery. Eden McCallum, as a firm, was designed with a center core of traditional employees whom they called partners. But these partners weren't expected to work on projects: instead, they were responsible for developing and scoping work with clients and then partnering them with a team of consultants pulled from a network of independent contractors—the Eden McCallum talent pool.

When a new client signs on, Eden McCallum dives into its talent pool and builds a team around the project. In the beginning, the company would bring the client a list of names of people it recommended for the project, and the client would then choose who and how many people would be on the team.[4] Yet, as the company grew, they discovered that most clients preferred to have Eden McCallum make the people decisions and build the team. After all, it was Eden McCallum's partners who knew the talent pool the best. "We thought in the beginning," Eden recalled, "'Wouldn't it be great if you could pick your consultants?' We did that for a few years, but then as we got older clients actually turned around and said, 'You know, I trust you guys. Just tell me who you think should do it and who that team should be.'"[5]

The talent pool itself is impressive. The firm is rigorous in its hiring process, bringing into the pool only one out of every ten applicants.[6] Eden McCallum now boasts over 500 core consultants, with another 1,000 in their network. A majority of them are refugees from top consultancies looking for intellectually engaging work with more choice and control in terms of what they take on. About half of its talent pool uses Eden McCallum as their main source of income, while the other half are happy to work on as little as one project per year. These consultants have individually defined their terms of engagement with the firm, deciding on what sectors to work in, when they'll work, and even their willingness to travel. All of the consultants' expertise and their preferences are entered into a database as search terms that partners can use as they build a team.

Since the world of an independent contractor can be a lonely one at times, Eden McCallum takes steps to ensure that its talent pool feels more like a team. The firm conducts knowledge-sharing and informational events for consultants where they meet each other and share experiences, as well as obtain industry and firm updates. Many of these trainings are run by the consultants themselves, both as a means of keeping home office operations lean but also as a way to stimulate knowledge exchange among the consultants. These trainings not only build a sense of connection but also reinforce the idea that Eden McCallum is making a long-term commitment, even if it's not a full-time one. "We'll have knowledge-sharing events, sometimes we'll have talks from people in industry about a particular topic, and then there's also simple social events," Liann Eden explained. "That's a large part of being in a relationship, not just a transaction. It's important to really get to know them professionally, probably to a much greater extent than a traditional firm, at least in terms of what they're looking to get out of their career, and what projects and clients are going to really excite them."[7]

Combining interesting projects with a high-caliber talent pool has made for a strong performance by Eden McCallum. Founded in London, the company opened its first international office, in Amsterdam, in 2008. In 2015, it opened a new office in Zurich and is now planning to open an office in New York City. Although the firm started off contracting with smaller clients not traditionally pursued by the big firms, today its client list includes large companies such as Shell, InterContinental Hotels Group, and Asda Walmart.[8]

Eden McCallum is a consulting firm with no consultants and uses that to its competitive advantage. Its success can seem baffling, since it contradicts much of what we think we already know about organizational design — and in particular, the organizational chart.

Origins of Org Charts

Organizational charts are a fixture in the modern company. Even in small companies where everyone answers to the company founder, employees seem to instinctively draw out organizational charts, if only in their heads. The series of lines and boxes outlining who reports to whom is so commonplace that it's difficult to think of the org chart as a fairly recent invention. But that's exactly what it is — an invention — and exactly when it arrived — relatively recently.

The first organizational chart is dated around 1855.[9] Daniel Mc-

Callum (no affiliation with Eden McCallum), the superintendent of the New York and Erie Railway, began experimenting with a way to keep the 5,000 employees under his supervision informed and efficient. McCallum utilized the telegraph as a way to communicate information quickly and the organizational chart as a means for outlining who was responsible to whom.

McCallum's organizational chart, drawn by civil engineer George Holt Henshaw, looks very different from today's typical organizational chart. Instead, it looks a lot like a railroad map. More than a dozen lines spread out from a wheelhouse of senior managers, who occupy the bottom section of the diagram. Instead of top-down, the chains of command move outward and upward along the picture. These lines separate into branches and tributaries as the divisions get more complex. In the end, McCallum's chart outlined the entire scope of the railway's administrative duties and also the number and class of employees in each department. Combined with innovations in communication, it provided an efficient means by which information could travel throughout the New York and Erie Railway, and it is still considered a landmark innovation in management history.

In the early years, this innovation didn't spread very far beyond the railroad industry. A survey conducted in the 1920s showed that organizational charts seemed not to be in widespread use among ordinary businesses.[10] More than fifty years after its invention, the tool still hadn't scaled. However, by the organizational chart's 100th birthday, it could be found in almost every major company in America.

Organizational charts did exactly what they promised: they organized groups of people into clear and concise reporting relationships. Assuming that the nature of the work didn't change and that employees completed the same tasks every day, the org chart made it possible to estimate how many employees were needed for daily tasks and how much supervision those employees needed. Personnel directors could assess the work needs of a department, write up a job description, and find someone to perform the specific bundle of tasks needed.

The Ever-Changing Org Chart

Assuming that the collective value of all of those tasks (all of the jobs in the company) was worth more to those outside the organization than the cost of performing them, the organizational chart ensured that the company stayed in business. As long as the nature of the work didn't change, the organizational chart didn't need changing. And for a long time it was possible to work one's entire career in an organization and climb the organizational chart without ever witnessing it change; at most, it might change only slightly. But eventually things did change. The very nature of work changed — from manual work to what Peter Drucker famously labeled "knowledge work." Knowledge work was much harder to predict and organize because the tasks and work effort required changed much more often than was the case with manual work.

As Roger Martin, former dean at the Rotman School of Management in Toronto, points out in an article for *Harvard Business Review,* the difficulty in prediction can actually make the organizational chart less efficient, not more so.[11] When the basic units of labor are jobs (a collection of repeatable tasks), planning the right number of people and where they should go on the organizational chart is easy. The flow of work is smooth, and the same tasks are repeated every day. But when the basic unit of labor is knowledge work (research, discussions, and so on), planning the right number of people is much more difficult because the flow of work isn't smooth. Martin argues that this random kind of workload often creates excess capacity and even fuels the cycle of layoffs and rapid hiring that seem to follow from economic depressions and recoveries.

However, if the basic unit is the project instead of the job and people are reassigned to different roles and projects depending on needs, then excess capacity is reduced and overhead and fixed costs are lowered. Layoffs might even be avoided. "The key to breaking the binge-and-purge cycle in knowledge work is to use the project rather than the job as the organizing principle," Martin writes. "In this model, employees are seen not as tethered to certain specified functions but as flowing to projects where their capabilities are needed."[12]

It's worth pointing out that most consulting firms operate slightly more on a project basis than the industrial companies that birthed the organizational chart. However, they still struggle with capacity problems and getting the right number of people to the right job. Even consulting firms struggle with rewriting the organizational chart quickly enough. Eden McCallum, by essentially writing the organizational chart in pencil, erasing it, and rewriting it quickly, is able to take advantage of Martin's insight and doesn't have to worry about whether employees are working at full capacity. That difference in capacity is why Eden McCallum can offer a match at a lower cost. According to Roger Martin, when companies adopt a project-focus organizational design, they "can cut the numbers of knowledge workers they have on payroll because they can move the ones they have around. The result is less downtime and make-work."[13]

Clay Christensen, the theorist behind the concept of "disruptive innovation," even labeled Eden McCallum as one of the companies disrupting management consulting.[14] It was Eden McCallum's fluid structure that allowed it to become such a disruptive force. With its network of independent consultants, instead of full-time, hierarchy-climbing employees, the firm keeps a low overhead and has relatively small fixed costs. In the early days, those low costs allowed the firm to work with smaller companies with smaller budgets.[15] In the beginning, the average project brought in about $75,000. As the firm's reputation grew, however, so did the size of the clients that pursued it. Today Eden McCallum's typical project budget is $250,000 to $400,000, with many projects going over $1.5 million.

Because of its smaller beginnings, the firm developed a reputation for providing Big Three–caliber consultants but at much lower prices to small and midsize firms. Shortly after the firm entered the Dutch market, an article in the Dutch financial newspaper *Financieele Dagblad* ran with the headline: "Eden McCallum Delivers Ex-McKinsey and Ex-BCG People at Half the Price."[16]

The Dutch newspaper's description of Eden McCallum's value proposition made its partners uncomfortable. In their minds, and in the minds of most of their long-term clients, it wasn't just that the fluid organizational structure provided a lean operation and a lower cost. By writing their organizational chart in pencil and then rewriting it as new projects came up, Eden McCallum had also found a way to provide a better-quality consulting experience — one that tapped into its high-level talent and drew out even higher-quality work than its consultants had produced when they were employed by the Big Three. "Every single project team is selected based on what's right for the project," Liann Eden explained. "They are also choosing to do each project — so we get 100 percent commitment."[17]

The Organizational Network

To understand the true value of this new way to write an organizational chart, we have to leave the executive boardrooms of high-level consulting and move to the world of Broadway. Specifically, we investigate the teams that bring a Broadway musical from idea to reality.

Every Broadway production is created and run by a senior leadership team with the same seats at the table, but who sits in those seats and how they got to them can tell us a lot about the best way to staff projects and design organizations. The senior leadership team of every show consists of about six roles — producer, director, composer, lyricist, librettist, and choreographer. Broadway as an industry, however, is a very small world. It is an amazingly dense and interconnected network, with different people often rotating to new roles as new shows are produced. As a result, the people in these roles sometimes find themselves working with total strangers but at other times find that their new team has several familiar faces. This constant churn caught the attention of two researchers, Brian Uzzi of Northwestern University and Jarrett Spiro of INSEAD.[18]

The duo was interested in discovering the right mix of connections for a team, and hence the right level of connectedness for Broadway as a whole. "It's well known that people in the industry form long-term partnerships with one another and these partnerships repeat themselves in different musicals," Uzzi explained. "What we were looking for is, how are these partnerships imbedded, so to speak, in a larger web of relationships that goes beyond just the team that someone worked with and into how that team was connected to other teams?"[19]

To answer this question, Uzzi and Spiro collected reports on every six-person leadership team from every Broadway show from 1945 to 1989.[20] They even included shows that were started but killed in preproduction. In the end, they built a database of 474 musicals and more than 2,000 individuals, from unknown choreographers to legendary composers such as Cole Porter and Andrew Lloyd Webber.

Using the database, the researchers could re-create the network of the Broadway industry spanning over four decades and calculate the levels of connectedness for any given year. They then analyzed the density of the network from year to year using a measurement they called a "small world Q," or simply "Q." Q measures the level of interconnectedness in a network on a scale from 1 to 5. A loose network with very few preexisting relationships and little familiarity between network members would have a Q score of 1, while the densest possible network, one in which everyone knows and has worked with everyone else, would have a Q score of 5.

Using the Q scores, they analyzed the success and failure of a given year on Broadway (judged by critical acclaim and financial success) and the extent to which networks affected Broadway's overall success. The result was astounding. The Q score — and hence the networks — had a tremendous effect on success, but it wasn't linear. As the Q score of a production year rose, so did that year's success rates, but it only rose so far before the success rates started dropping again. Instead of a straight line, Uzzi and Spiro got an inverted U, with the peak success rate hovering around 2.6 on the Q scale of 1 to 5.

What this meant was that a team of total strangers usually wasn't very successful, but neither was a team of strongly familiar colleagues. The best years on Broadway were marked by teams with a combination of somewhat close connections and new perspectives. "Broadway as an industry works best when things are connected to each other but there is also enough space that the creative material can flow and go to different people at different times," Uzzi explained.[21] As teams with this combination tackle the challenges involved in producing a show, they benefit not only from the experiences and social norms of their known colleagues but also from the diverse perspectives and new ideas of newbies.

It's tempting to read the results of Uzzi and Spiro's study and assume that the key to success is merely to build project teams that combine old colleagues with newcomers. But the study isn't about the team — *it's about the network*. It's the network of Broadway that allows 2.6 teams to form, produce a show, and then disband into new teams. If you build a 2.6 team and force it to work together for a long time, it ceases to be a 2.6 team and moves toward becoming a 5 team. Instead, you need to focus on the overall network so that you can create the right-combination team around a project but you can also reassign its members quickly to new projects and new teams.

This is the problem with organizational charts that stay stale for too long. Besides capacity issues and overhead costs, organizational charts outline who is on what team, and that won't change until the organizational chart changes. By writing its organizational chart in pencil — by making a fluid network instead of a stale hierarchy — Eden McCallum can form new teams around projects and then reshuffle teams when the projects are over. "It's always a bit of a mixture," Liann Eden said, describing Eden McCallum's consulting teams. "There are consultants who have worked together before and some who are new."[22] By building a system of independent consultants, Eden McCallum has built a network that runs similarly to the best-performing production years on Broadway.

Eden McCallum isn't the only company to have done this, and they're not the first. In fact, many companies have structured themselves in a way that allows them to hire full-time employees and still organize them around projects instead of around positions on an inflexible organizational chart.

The employees of SumAll, in addition to having totally transparent salaries, also have very fluid job assignments. Employees' positions in the organization depend on what they're working on at the time. The company organizes around projects instead of products. Founder Dane Atkinson and an appointed committee settle on the strategy and objectives for the year and then empower employees to start new projects so long as those projects are aligned with the strategy. "New products come complete from employee teams," said Atkinson.[23]

Teams build around those projects and self-elect a leader. Then they go to work on the project. When it's completed, or when an individual's contribution to the project is finished, the team then gets reshuffled. Sometimes teams make trades based on their skill needs. "There's a little bit of horse-trading going on between team leaders at times," Atkinson said. "The average person changes teams once or twice a year"— which is far more frequently than if SumAll had built the organizational chart around set products and kept people permanently assigned to their teams.

By creating this project-based format, SumAll has set up a structure similar to the social network of Broadway or the talent pool of Eden McCallum, but using full-time employees instead of independent contractors. As a result, the teams at SumAll are kept well balanced between folks who have worked together before and newbies with new perspectives. By abandoning the traditional organizational chart, SumAll has organized around a network that would probably score somewhere close to 2.6 on the small world Q scale. In other words, it would have a most beneficial score.

Eden McCallum and SumAll are perfect examples of the benefits of a project-based organizational chart, but again, they are hardly the first ones to try it. One company has been writing its organizational chart in pencil since it was founded in 1958: W. L. Gore. The creator of GoreTex fabric as well as equally innovative products like Elixir Guitar Strings and Glide dental floss, Gore was founded around the idea that it could better tap into the innovation talents of its people if it created what founder Bill Gore called a "lattice, not a hierarchy," with every employee connected to every other employee. Just as at SumAll, Gore employees propose and volunteer for new projects and rotate around as projects change. As projects draw to a close, employees begin looking for the next place to jump in and help, thus keeping the network capable of refreshing the diversity of teams. Gore has used this model throughout the almost sixty years in which it has grown from Bill Gore's basement to a 10,000-person company with offices on three continents and more than $3 billion in annual revenue.

Eden McCallum, SumAll, and W. L. Gore all represent radical attempts to continuously redraw the organizational chart. By contrast, the well-known design firm IDEO has sought to create a culture in which the organizational chart is relatively stable but people still feel free to move around to assist various projects.[24]

The root of this culture at IDEO probably began in the mid-1990s. IDEO, then only a few years old, had grown rapidly from a small design studio to around 150 people who all reported directly to the original senior team. The company needed a reorganization that would make the firm more efficient but also preserve the collaborative benefits of the small design company. Instead of locking himself away and creating a master diagram, as Daniel McCallum did, IDEO founder David Kelley decided to let the organizational chart develop organically. Kelley called a meeting and explained to everyone that, instead of one big organizational flow chart, they would instead be working in and around five leaders, with each heading a new "studio."

The leaders then took turns speaking about the type of work they preferred, the challenges they faced, and what was exciting about their approach to design and innovation.[25] The meeting ended with Kelley asking employees to list which leader they'd like to work with and which project they'd like to work on. Employees were asked to rank their first, second, and third preferences. As a result, instead of leaders picking their team and plotting them on the organizational chart, IDEO employees got to choose their leader. As it turned out, everyone got their first choice.

As they were reorganizing, however, Kelley reminded everyone that one of the firm's guiding principles was "enlightened trial and error": even with this new structure, their assignments and their preferences were all a prototype and would change as needed. "The changes we are trying to make," Kelley told the group, ". . . are temporary and reversible experiments."[26] A few years later, after the company had grown even more, IDEO shuffled everything again and repeated the process, allowing employees to once again pick their place on the organizational chart around studio leaders.[27] David Kelley and the team at IDEO treated the organizational chart as a prototype, on the principle that trying to organize individuals shouldn't block them from collaborating and doing great work.

Nearly twenty years later, this unique philosophy continues to permeate IDEO's culture despite its expansion to more than 500 employees scattered across ten offices worldwide. Although the expansion has led to a bigger organizational chart, employees are still encouraged to branch off from their place in the hierarchy and help another team on a project. In fact, it is so encouraged that IDEO gives employees a certain amount of time in their workweek to dedicate to helping other project teams.

In a study of IDEO's culture led by Teresa Amabile of the Harvard Business School, researchers found that collaboration and helping others, even those outside of their project, form a regular part of how employees get work done at IDEO. "Most people at IDEO learn to do it as they become steeped in the culture of the organization, participate in its regular activities, and develop networks within the firm," the researchers wrote.[28] To study these networks, the researchers mapped one office at IDEO by asking employees who had helped them on projects and who the top five helpers in the organization were. Amazingly, every single employee was named as a helper by at least one other person in the company. In addition, 89 percent of all employees showed up on someone else's list of the top five helpers. The researchers even witnessed firsthand a member of the senior team using his helping time to jump into a brainstorming session for a team whose project hadn't even formally begun.

IDEO's organizational chart isn't as malleable as the ones at Eden McCallum, SumAll, and W. L. Gore. Even in its early years, however, the company has reinforced the notion that the organizational chart isn't hard doctrine. It encourages employees to branch out beyond their formal teams to produce better collaborations and keep the network humming (though probably unintentionally) somewhere around 2.6 on the small world Q scale. In doing so, IDEO is an example of a company benefiting from the power of network culture even if it isn't free to rewrite its organizational chart around projects.

To abuse the analogy, just because you can't write the organizational chart in pencil doesn't mean that you can't write it in erasable pen.

10

■

CLOSE OPEN OFFICES

While the recent trend toward open offices is often explained as necessary to inspire collaboration, research and experience have shown that the benefits of open office design for collaboration are typically offset by myriad distractions. The best leaders have a different answer for the open- versus closed-office debate.

I N THE MID-1990S, Jay Chiat pushed his office to the farthest reaches of open office design. Chiat founded his company, now called TBWA/Chiat/Day, as a one-man advertising agency.[1] From the very beginning, his company found success on a grand scale. Chiat quickly merged with Guy Day to form Chiat/Day. (Chiat got his name first, while Guy got to be president.)

Together they collaborated on some of the most memorable advertising campaigns in history. Chiat oversaw the creation and production of the famous Apple "1984" Super Bowl commercial, which featured a young female runner hurling a sledgehammer through a gigantic television screen where Big Brother was lecturing workers in a dystopian future. Chiat followed that up with Apple's equally famous "Think Different" campaign. He also created the Energizer Bunny for Eveready Batteries and other notable brand icons. In 1990, *Advertising Age* magazine labeled his company "the agency of the decade."

As Chiat turned his attention to the workplace — and his workplace in particular — he sought to explore another revolutionary idea. In the spring of 1993, while skiing down the slopes of Telluride in Colorado, Chiat considered how the workplace affects work. He reflected on how work spaces are often designed simply as a reflection of the corporate hierarchy and politics, with offices getting bigger and more isolated the higher up an employee moves. "You go to work and you only leave your office when you have to go to the bathroom," Chiat told *Wired* magazine in an interview about his new office design. "That sort of thing breeds insularity and fear, and it's nonproductive." He also thought about how technology was eliminating the need to even be at the office all of the time. (This was, after all, near the height of the first dot-com bubble.) By the time Chiat was done with his ski run, he'd had an epiphany. He was going to fundamentally redesign the offices of Chiat/Day as an example to the world of how business should be done.

Later that year Chiat presented his plan to the public. In short, Chiat would tear down all of the walls and cubicles of his West Coast office, removing all of the desks and desktop computers as well. Everything that might cause an individual employee to become territorial would be removed. "What you get when you come into work is a locker — and a computer and phone that you can check out for the day," Chiat said. Employees would take that laptop computer and cell phone and find a place to work among a myriad of tables, desks, and couches in one giant room. Any personal effects, family pictures, or personal awards could be kept in the locker, but they weren't tolerated in the "team workroom." Chiat had pushed his entire company to the farthest edges of what he saw as the future of work—the most open of open offices.

There was just one problem. It didn't work.

Within a year of the redesign, news had reached the public about how far off Chiat's design had been.[2] Instead of preventing office politics, the new design heightened it, and turf wars sprouted up between employees over areas and tools intended for common use. Some employees would arrive early in the morning, check out a laptop and phone, then hide them away in their lockers and sleep for a few more hours before starting work. Others would hide their computers overnight so that they could keep using the same one the next day. Since no one was allowed to leave anything out in the common area, they began stuffing unfinished work into their lockers, which were far too small to hold everything. One woman began putting all of her things in a toy red wagon in order to keep track of it all.

Worst of all, the common area wasn't big enough for everyone. The open space wasn't spacious enough. People would arrive for the day and find no place to work, so they would leave. Managers wouldn't be able to bring a whole team together. Work wasn't getting done. By 1998, Chiat/Day had realized that Chiat's epiphany about an open office space wasn't such a good idea. They were forced to redesign again, this time creating almost the opposite of Chiat's Telluride vision. They cleared out of the old office and moved the entire company to a different, more traditionally designed office space.

While Chiat's experiment had failed, word of his failure didn't spread as far as word of the original trial. In fact, numerous leaders of various companies had heard about the wide-open office, and some of them had followed suit. Ernst & Young mimicked the "hoteling" aspect of unassigned desks for its frequently traveling workers. Sprint and Cisco Systems both tried to design a more "virtual office." In fact, the pace of the march toward open offices hasn't slowed despite several experiments that were demonstrable failures. Even more amazing is that the march seemed to pick up the pace in 2000 and 2008, when recessions made open floor plans a far cheaper and hence far more appealing option for corporations.

These days, 70 percent of American workplaces have an open office environment, and new business leaders have replaced Jay Chiat as the standard bearers.[3] When Michael Bloomberg became mayor of New York City, he famously moved out of the mayor's office and into the center cubicle in a cavernous space of fifty low-partitioned desks packed together. Bloomberg swore by "the bullpen" and the benefits of its lack of privacy. How Bloomberg used his office space has become a subject of study for heads of government and the future heads of companies studying in MBA classrooms.[4] In 2015, Mark Zuckerberg announced that Facebook would create the largest open office in the world. The social network even hired the renowned architect Frank Gehry to design a 430,000-square-foot building to house 2,800 employees in one giant room.[5]

Overall, this trend shrank the average space per employee from 500 square feet in the 1970s to just 200 square feet in 2010.[6] While that space comes with an undeniable cost savings, advocates for the open office believe that the biggest benefit is increased collaboration and better communication among employees, which in turn creates greater productivity.

That claim, however, is very deniable. A wealth of studies on open office plans suggests that the benefits of open offices probably fail to outweigh the costs.

Open Offices Shut Employees Down

Shortly after Jay Chiat's office experiment, another more rigorous experiment around workplace design was undertaken. A western Canada–based oil and gas company was redesigning its offices and transitioning from a traditional office space to an open floor plan. The company's leaders asked a team of psychologists from the nearby University of Calgary to study the effect of the transition on employees.[7]

The researchers held several focus groups to determine what should be measured and how to take those measurements. They created a survey to measure employees' attitudes about their physical environment, stressors, team member relations, office protocols, and performance. They then had managers distribute surveys to employees with instructions to seal the survey after answering it and mail it directly to the researchers (to protect anonymity). The surveys were distributed just prior to the transition, one month after moving to the new open office, and six months after the move.

After they'd collected and analyzed all of the data from the surveys, the researchers found that employees appeared to be negatively affected *in every measurement* by the new open office layout. The employees reported decreases in satisfaction with their environment, worsening relationships with team members, and lower perceived job performance. They also reported an increase in physical stress. Moreover, the researchers found that these responses were still present at the six-month observation point, implying that even after employees had adjusted to the new environment, the negative effects remained. In fact, satisfaction with team member relations continued to decline and was lowest six months after the move.

The results of the study certainly implied that changing to an open office floor plan weakened productivity and increased stress, but the researchers acknowledged that their sample size was quite low (only twenty-one employees completed all three surveys). However, further research with much larger samples would reinforce their observations.

In 2005, Jungsoo Kim and Richard de Dear from the University of Sydney conducted a study using a much larger data set and sample size.[8] These researchers collected data on office environments from the industry standard of work environment research, the Post-Occupancy Evaluation (POE) database at the University of California at Berkeley. Since its inception in 2000, the POE has become one of the most widely used assessments of office space. (It's even utilized for LEED-certification assessments.) Its widespread use has resulted in a massive amount of data for researchers.

Kim and de Dear selected a small subset of the data based on office building categories, which was still quite massive: 42,764 observations collected from 303 office buildings. They classified each building into one of five categories, ranging from enclosed private offices to open offices with no partitions, and then compared satisfaction levels across categories on a variety of dimensions such as noise level, sound privacy, ease of interaction, comfort of furnishing, air quality, temperature, and even amount of light.

Unsurprisingly, they found that enclosed private offices had the overall highest satisfaction rate and that open office plans had the lowest. But it was when they looked at individual dimensions that they found a few surprises. The biggest differences between private offices and open-plan offices were in dimensions such as visual privacy, sound privacy, amount of space, and noise level. A lack of sound privacy received the most negative responses from employees in open offices. In addition, between 25 and 30 percent of employees in open-plan offices were dissatisfied with the level of noise in their workplace. However, satisfaction with ease of interaction was no higher in open offices than in private offices. Thus, while noise was a problem, the greater noise level didn't appear to be from all of the collective collaboration buzzing around the open room.

The researchers then took their analysis one step further, using regression to calculate how important each dimension was to employees' overall satisfaction. One of the dimensions most strongly related to overall satisfaction was ease of interaction, despite the fact that it was judged to be no better or worse in open office plans than in private offices. In other words, the desire for more collaboration among employees was shared by all, but those in open office plans may not have found it to be worth all of the stress and distraction from the bombardment of noise.

In 2011, three professors from the University of Leeds had results similar to those of the Calgary researchers, even when the perception of the open office was initially positive.[9] Matthew Davis, Desmond Leach, and Chris Clegg compiled and summarized the results of over 100 individual studies on office environment. They found that open office plans do succeed in making employees *feel* like they are part of a more innovative and collaborative environment. However, the open floor plan is also damaging to employees' productivity, attention span, satisfaction, and creative thinking because it creates more interruptions, heightens stress, and makes employees less able to concentrate. It's interesting to note their finding that open offices do increase collaboration (or at least appear to), but the overall benefits of that collaboration don't seem to offset the costs to productivity and innovation.

Inside the lab, Gary Evans and Dana Johnson of Cornell University found the same effect of open office noise on stress.[10] Forty female clerical workers responded to their advertisement requesting volunteers to participate in a research project on computer workstation equipment. (Some men responded to the advertisement, but because the majority turned out to be women, the researchers decided to limit the study to women to control for possible gender differences.) Each woman was randomly assigned to one of two conditions: a quiet office or a noisy office. Each woman participated in two three-hour-long sessions — one to set a baseline, and the other for the experiment itself. During the experimental session, the women were asked to type text from an aviation safety manual into a computer at what would be a normal, relaxed pace for them. The women were told that the researchers were not monitoring their performance (although the researchers actually were).

The women in the noisy office condition were asked to type while low-level sounds simulated an actual open office (ringing phones, typing sounds, and drawers being opened and closed), while the women in the quiet condition were not. As would be realistic in any office environment, all of the women were interrupted every twenty-five minutes and asked to complete quick tasks. The researchers tracked their typing performance and also observed how often the women in either condition made adjustments to their workstation. (Making regular ergonomic changes to posture and workstations has been shown to reduce the risk of musculoskeletal diseases.)

After the session, researchers also measured the epinephrine, norepinephrine, and cortisol levels of the women to get accurate markers of stress. Lastly, all participants were given a variety of puzzles (some solvable and some unsolvable) and told to work on one puzzle at a time until they either solved it or decided that it couldn't be solved. Then they could go on to the next one if time allowed.

The participants in both conditions averaged the same levels of performance, and neither group reported feeling any more stressed than the other at the end of the experimental session, but their epinephrine levels suggested that the noisy environment did cause significant stress. In addition, the women in the noisy condition made significantly fewer changes to their workstation, suggesting that the noisy environment was negatively affecting their future health. Moreover, the women in the noisy condition made significantly fewer attempts to solve the puzzles, indicative of decreased motivation after exposure to the noisy environment. Evans and Johnson's findings suggest that immediate performance might not be dampened by an open office environment, but that increased stress, decreased motivation, and illness might accumulate to reduce overall productivity later on.

Evans and Johnson simply suggested that noise from open offices can cause illness in employees, but researchers in Denmark found that employees who work in open floor plans really do get sick more often.[11] Using a national survey, the Danish Work Environment Cohort Study—four researchers led by Jan Pejtersen—studied a sample of Danish citizens who reported spending most of their work time inside an office. The researchers divided the 2,403 respondents' workplaces into one of four types of office: a private office, an office shared with one colleague, an office shared with three to six colleagues, and an open-plan office.

Pejtersen and his colleagues analyzed how the office type changed the response to a simple question: "In total, how many sick days have you taken in the last year?" Because the sample was part of a larger national survey, they were able to control for age, gender, smoking habits, physical activity, body mass, and just about any other variable that would affect illness. They found that individuals in private offices reported taking the least number of sick days. Individuals who occupied a shared office with another colleague took 50 percent more sick days than private office occupants, and those who worked in open office plans took 62 percent more sick days. (Strangely, those who shared an office with three to six people reported only 36 percent more sick days than private office residents.)

Although the study was not designed to prove that open offices make people sick, the results are strongly indicative that this is the case. In addition, since the researchers were unable to verify each illness, it could also be that the open office occupants in their study simply didn't want to come into work. Nonetheless, the sheer size of the study reveals that open offices are occupied far less often by the productive employees who are supposed to be collaborating in them.

Workspace That Works

The decades of research into office layouts do provide one glimmer of hope for open office employees, or at least a way to counter some of the negative effects. In 2005, two researchers, So Young Lee of Yonsei University and Jay Brand of the office furniture company Haworth (himself a cognitive psychologist), collaborated on a study of the effect of perceived control of the workspace on employees' satisfaction.[12] They found that control does indeed have a strong effect on employee satisfaction.

They studied 228 employees from five American organizations ranging from a Midwest auto supplier to a Southwest telecommunications firm. The offices that the participants worked in varied across four types, from private offices to completely open-plan offices. The participants were given a thirty-nine-item questionnaire designed to assess the level of distractions, the flexible use of workspace, perceived control, job performance, job satisfaction, teamwork, and individuals' inclination to seek out private or public workspaces. Unsurprisingly, they found that participants who reported high levels of distraction also reported lower levels of satisfaction with their work environment.

But surprisingly, employees who felt that they had personal control over their physical work environment (being able to change the arrangement of their desk or move to a different space to work when they wanted to) reported that they were more satisfied with their office environment, more cohesive with their team, and more satisfied with their jobs. Those who were more satisfied with their jobs also performed better.

Lee and Brand's study suggests that the real question might not be open or closed, but *how much control* companies allow employees to have over where and how they work. Even an open office might be tolerable (and maybe even enjoyable) if employees are given some level of individual control. These findings have also been shared by the designers and architects looking to create the best possible office (inside the constraints of costs). Creating the best workplace might not require closing open offices or opening up closed ones. It might not be an either-or choice.

"Good workplaces ultimately give people a little bit of both. They push them to be together part of the time, and they give them the option or ability to be independent or isolated part of the time," said David Craig.[13] Craig is a workplace strategist at CannonDesign and holds a PhD in architecture and cognitive science. "A lot of organizations have tried to just get away from the idea of having any kind of dedicated space, creating workplaces that are a mix of all of the above and giving people the freedom to work wherever they want." As empirical evidence suggests, designing that mix and letting employees choose seems to be the best option. Jay Chiat wasn't that far off when he wanted Chiat/Day staff to choose where they worked every day. He was just way off in limiting their choices to an open desk or a different open desk.

That choice and openness is what Alexander Saint-Amand sought to offer the employees of Gerson Lehrman Group, Inc. (GLG), a consulting firm with a unique business model that pairs individual experts with individuals seeking aid for one-to-one consulting.[14] Given the firm's unique business model, Saint-Amand wanted something totally different for his employees. In 2014 GLG moved its headquarters into a brand-new space at One Grand Central Place in New York City.

The two-story headquarters begins in a giant, light-filled atrium with furniture designed to look like a living room. What is unique about the space, however, is that the relaxed living room feel never gives way to a sea of cubicles or rows of desks. Instead, the entire space is a collection of various furniture types with a large coffee shop in the center of the first floor. In addition to the café stools and living room couches and chairs in the atrium, the office furnishings range from open tables to library-style carrels, to conference rooms big enough for large groups or small enough for just one person seeking solace.

Employees at GLG don't have an assigned desk. As with Chiat/Day's experimental office, they have a locker to store personal effects and are given the freedom to roam anywhere they want in the two-story space. Unlike Chiat/Day, everyone gets a laptop computer, and there is enough space for everyone. The new design covers 65,000 square feet and can hold 350 people; GLG only employs 250. In addition, the office is organized around "neighborhoods" that are outfitted with printers, copiers, and other equipment. There is a neighborhood for each business unit, so deskless employees always feel like they have a territory or home base. In addition, employees who are used to traditional desktop computers can plug their laptops into specialized desks with keyboards, mouses, and large-screen monitors.

What is most interesting about GLG's office is that, to the un-initiated, it looks like the traditional open office environment. But the diversity of options and unlimited choices provide the benefits of the open office with the added benefit of individual control that Lee and Brand found in their research. That level of control would not be possible in a more traditional office setting. "We want you to feel like you own the whole office, not just your desk," said architect Clive Wilkinson. "That's a landmark change because employees typically are kept in their place and told, 'If you're incredibly lucky, you might get an office one day.'"[15] Wilkinson, as fate would have it, was also the architect Jay Chiat hired after his own office experiment was deemed a failure.

Perhaps learning from Chiat's experience, Wilkinson made sure that the transitioning GLG employees felt that they had some control over not only the new design but the design process. The company created an architectural committee with representatives from each department and held regular town hall meetings with the entire staff to provide updates and get feedback. "You're really asking for trouble if you don't carry your staff along with you," Wilkinson said.[16]

Their final design extended that choice and control to employees indefinitely, providing them with a variety of different furnishings and giving them freedom to roam all day. "If they want to work at a desk, we have plenty of desk space," Saint-Amand explained. "If they want to work in a café or in teams or on couches, we have that space. If they need a private phone booth or a meeting room, we have all of that."[17] Even if employees want all of the above all day long, the extra space accommodates their personal choices and gives them control of those choices throughout the day. One staffer might start her day at the coffee shop meeting with colleagues from another department, then come back to her neighborhood to meet with her team, then retreat to a telephone booth–sized individual conference room to work quietly alone. Even Saint-Amand finds himself roaming throughout the day and alighting at various workspaces. The flexibility to roam provides the benefits not only of collaboration and ease of interaction but also of peace and quiet for those who are more easily distracted by the noisy areas of the office.

True, GLG's office is not the optimal design for every workplace, but its design demonstrates a viable solution to the question of how open or closed to make an office space. As Saint-Amand and Wilkinson believe, and as Jay Chiat ultimately learned, it comes down to what space is best for employees and the nature of their work. Any design that provides employees with maximum control over their personal workspace is better than a design that is completely closed or open.

In sum, open offices need to be closed and closed offices need to be opened, and employees need to be given choices that enable them to find what works best for them, for the team, and for the company.

11

■

TAKE SABBATICALS

Despite the temptation to be "always on," the best leaders give themselves and their employees a good long break once in a while — a sabbatical. These leaders have found that the best way to stay productive all of the time is to spend a good portion of the time being deliberately unproductive.

I N JULY 2009, the acclaimed artist and designer Stefan Sagmeister took the stage at the annual TEDGlobal conference and launched a counterintuitive idea.

At TEDGlobal, an annual gathering of the world's top thinkers and doers, speakers present "ideas worth spreading" to an audience that can most certainly help their work gain traction. Given the achievements of those assembled, Sagmeister's talk must have been met initially with surprise. His idea worth spreading was simple: *work less.* Sagmeister told his audience that he completely closes down his design studio every seven years and gives himself and his designers an entire year for personal travel and experimentation. He and his entire staff are free to pursue whatever interests them as long as it does not involve business as usual. "In that year, we are not available for any of our clients," he said. "We are totally closed."[1]

Sagmeister clearly knew his audience and knew they would find his message counterintuitive. Without being asked, he addressed what was certainly the obvious and most common question among his listeners: how could he afford to take so much time away? In a highly competitive world, where he and his company were only as good as their last project, wasn't it risky to leave behind his current projects, suspend his business relationships, and step away from his work entirely?

Sagmeister believes that quite the opposite is true — that stepping away from a successful career is, in fact, what has allowed him to have such a successful career. "That is clearly enjoyable for myself," he told the audience, "but probably more important . . . the work that comes out of this year flows back into the company and into society at large." Sagmeister found that, after his first sabbatical, all of his new projects were of much higher quality and directly related to his time off. "Basically, everything we've done in the seven years following the first sabbatical came out of [the] thinking of that one single year."[2] Since these ideas turned into higher-quality projects, his studio was able to charge even higher prices once the designers reassembled in New York after their year on leave. Sagmeister's experience was that the combination of rest and experimentation that came from the sabbaticals taken by him and his team refired their creativity, which, in turn, refueled their company's financial success.

Sabbatical programs are rare inside of corporate America, but their number is increasing. In a 2009 survey by the Society for Human Resource Management, fewer than 5 percent of companies in the United States offered *paid* sabbaticals.[3] By 2014 that number had climbed to 15 percent (3 percent offering paid leave and another 12 percent offering unpaid sabbaticals).[4] But even though they might seem like a new idea to the companies that adopt them, sabbaticals aren't exactly a new concept. The very word "sabbatical" is derived from the Hebrew word "Sabbath," an ancient concept of allowing for a time of rest at fixed intervals.

In the academic realm, sabbaticals are practically an institution. The first university to offer sabbaticals was the University of Sydney in the 1860s.[5] In the 1880s, sabbaticals reached the United States when Harvard instituted paid research leave, originally as a means to lure prominent scholars to campus. Over the next forty years, dozens of other top-level universities around the world followed suit. By the 1920s, a total of around fifty of the world's top collegiate institutions, including Oxford and Cambridge, were offering sabbatical leave.[6] Today sabbaticals are a fixed part of almost every academic institution, even though their availability may wax and wane with the economic conditions. Typically, universities offer professors one semester of full-paid leave, or a year at half-pay, to rejuvenate and also to conduct research. Faculty are usually eligible every six or seven years to apply for such a leave.

Even inside for-profit companies, sabbaticals have been around for a long time. The first corporate sabbatical program in the United States was most likely offered by McDonald's in 1977.[7] Initially, the program offered eight weeks of paid leave for every ten years of employment and applied to everyone employed directly by the company (but not those employed by a franchise owner), including senior executives, managers of company-owned restaurants, and even maintenance staff. Given the tens of thousands of people McDonald's employs, there are thousands of employees on sabbatical in any given year. In addition to serving more hamburgers than any other restaurant, McDonald's has also handed out more sabbaticals than any other corporation.

In 2006 McDonald's quickened the pace, adding a one-week

mini-sabbatical for every five years of service. Beyond just rest and relaxation, McDonald's leaders have found that sabbaticals help with talent development and succession planning. "When people are not around for two months, you get a glimpse of how [their replacements] perform, so from a talent management standpoint, it has advantages," said Rich Floersch, the chief human resources officer at McDonald's.[8] Some employees who covered for their colleagues on leave have been promoted to new roles because of how good their coverage was.

Shortly after McDonald's adopted the program, leaders at Intel followed suit and became the first of what would be many technology companies known for the sabbatical benefit. In 1981, Intel rolled out its program, which qualifies employees to take eight weeks of paid leave (with full benefits) every seven years.[9] In addition, Intel allows employees to take that leave anytime within three years after qualifying, so that employees who need to align their sabbatical with a spouse's break or job transition are better able to do so. Intel also allows employees to add on up to four weeks of vacation time to extend their sabbatical out to nearly three months.

Like McDonald's, Intel has found that its program serves two purposes. "The primary purpose was for the employee to rejuvenate," said Tami Graham, the director of global benefits strategy for Intel. "The secondary purpose was for the development of others." Every sabbatical is also an opportunity for those who stay to be cross-trained to cover for the employee on sabbatical. Surprisingly, Graham also found that the cost to Intel was minimal compared to the benefits. "People are on the payroll whether they are there or not, and the work is being covered within the organization, so there's no real cost." But when rested employees return with new energy and the employees who covered for them develop new skills, everyone experiences the return on investment.

After Intel, a series of Silicon Valley firms began copying the practice, including Adobe, Autodesk, and Menlo Innovations.[10] The practice doesn't just work for big-name companies with large staffs. In 2012, Scott Heiferman, the founder and CEO of MeetUp, rolled out a sabbatical program for its seventy-five employees.[11] MeetUp is a smaller tech company whose main product is MeetUp .com, an online social network for planning offline group meetings. The program allows up to three months of paid leave after employees have been with the company for seven years. Heiferman launched the program initially as a retention strategy; seven years in the tech industry is practically a lifetime. "The way most folks get a nice, long break from work is if they leave their job and then scratch their itch and find a new job," said Brendan McGovern, Heiferman's cofounder and the first employee to take a sabbatical.

When McGovern took three months off, he found the rest and respite and "something new" he was looking for, but he also saw his time away as a developmental opportunity for his staff (the same way large companies like McDonald's and Intel use it). McGovern spent months briefing his team on how to cover for him, and they performed beautifully. "It really allowed people to step up and explore new areas," McGovern recalled.[12] In addition to rest and development, sabbaticals also gave MeetUp, a small company, a means to figure out how to grow organically. When one of the company's software engineers took a three-month sabbatical in Berlin, he returned to tell Heiferman and McGovern that he wanted to move there. So the founders developed a way for that engineer to open an office for MeetUp in Berlin and reach a new source of previously untapped talent.

Some companies have even experimented with offering sabbaticals earlier than after the traditional seven or ten years of employment. Morningstar, the Chicago-based investment research firm, offers employees sabbaticals as early as four years into their service. Founded in 1984 by Joe Mansueto, the firm has always been highly regarded for its casual and enjoyable work environment, which feels more like a California tech start-up than a Chicago investment company. In addition to rest, Morningstar uses the sabbatical as a way to reward and recognize employees. "We view the sabbatical program as a way of saying thanks for helping us grow while helping employees grow," the company's recruiting website boasts proudly.[13] Although not everyone takes a sabbatical when eligible, they still experience the positive effects of being offered one.[14]

Perhaps the most unique corporate sabbatical program ever launched was QuikTrip's. The chain of gasoline and convenience stores headquartered in Tulsa, Oklahoma, doesn't just offer paid sabbaticals to its executives. It *requires* them. It takes a long time to earn one, but the company mandates that all employees with twenty-five years of service take a four-week sabbatical. In addition, the company requires additional sabbaticals at thirty years, thirty-five years, and forty years of service. While twenty-five or forty years of service may seem like the right age for retirement, owing to QuikTrip's promote-from-within strategy and its retail environment, many long-tenured employees actually started with the company very young, working the cash registers at the store. Thus, twenty-five years is a good time to reward committed employees with a period of rest. "The purpose is to rejuvenate and to reduce burnout of tenured employees," said Kim Owen, the former vice president of human resources for QuikTrip.

Low Cost, High Return

If offering even unpaid sabbatical leave to employees seems like a stretch, the experiences of companies that offer paid leave or even *required* paid leave have shown that the overall cost is low and the return on investment is high. In addition to these experiences, a growing amount of research demonstrates the benefits of sabbaticals.

Since sabbaticals originated in the academic world, the majority of the research done on them has been conducted in that context. One of the more rigorous studies of sabbaticals came from a large group of researchers from the United States, Israel, and New Zealand. Twelve professors recently collaborated to study the effect of sabbaticals on coworkers at their ten universities.[15] James Campbell Quick, one of the authors of the study and a professor of organizational behavior at the University of Texas at Arlington, joined the research study after he took a sabbatical of sorts. Quick served three months in the Air Force Reserve. "I found that my time in the Air Force provided much-needed rejuvenation as well as complementary real-world experience to bring back to the classroom," Quick said.[16] When he returned from the service, Quick resolved to study the effects of sabbatical on the very aspects of it he had experienced.

Quick and the team surveyed 129 professors who qualified for sabbaticals in the upcoming academic semester. They then matched those 129 to a control set of 129 other faculty members with similar qualifications, tenure, and demographic information. The sabbatees and the control group were surveyed several times — one month before the sabbatical semester began, during the middle of the semester, and at the end of the semester. These surveys were designed to measure myriad factors, including perceived stress levels, psychological resources, and even life satisfaction.

After all the sabbatees had returned and the controls had finished the semester, the research team found that those who took sabbaticals did indeed experience a decline in stress and an increase in psychological resources and overall well-being.[17] In short, sabbaticals really did provide the respite and recharge that business leaders found their people experiencing.

Moreover, the effects of those positive changes often remained even after they returned to work, suggesting that the sabbatees and their organizations both gained significantly from the leave itself. "We discovered that a sabbatical affords the opportunity to acquire interpersonal and professional skills that you wouldn't have a chance to build otherwise," Quick explained.[18]

The research team also studied the differences, if any, between various types of sabbaticals. They found that those who fully detached themselves from their regular campus — skipping meetings, neglecting their offices, barely communicating with their university — gained the most from their sabbatical. In addition, those who spent their sabbatical in another country enjoyed bigger gains in well-being than did those who merely worked on different projects but from the same location.

Overall, the team's results suggest that sabbaticals really do provide a strong return on investment, not only for those leaving but for the company sending them away. Sabbatical leave promotes well-being, decreases stress, and provides opportunities to acquire new knowledge and skills. This is exactly what the business leaders who offer corporate sabbaticals have found.

Sabbaticals as Leadership Development

What about the effects of sabbatical leave on leadership development and succession? It turns out that question has been studied as well, and the results suggest that sabbaticals are good not just for future leaders but also for the leaders who take leave.

Two researchers, Deborah Linnell and Tim Wolfred, studied the effect of sabbaticals on leaders of nonprofit organizations.[19]

The duo surveyed sixty-one leaders at five foundations with sabbatical leave programs. Although the different organizations had different programs with different requirements, such as length of tenure or position required for sabbatical, all five programs had several characteristics in common. All required their sabbatees to take three to four months fully off and discouraged them from visiting the office. All required some post-sabbatical reflection, and all were created as a means to alleviate stress and the demands of the leadership role.

Although their results certainly showed that the sabbaticals were a stress reliever, there were also notable findings about the effect of time away on the leadership role itself. The researchers found that the majority of leaders surveyed had greater confidence in their role upon return and felt that the sabbatical allowed them to "think outside the box" and to generate new ideas for effecting change and raising funds for their organization. In addition, the majority found that they were better able to crystallize the existing vision for the organization and to create a new, more powerful one. They also reported being better able to work with their board of directors, as the planning and learning stages of the sabbatical process made directors more effective.

Most intriguingly, the researchers found that, for the majority of leaders, the interim leaders who filled in for them during their leave were more effective and responsible when their boss returned. Many interim leaders even continued in a more collaborative role with the senior leaders post-sabbatical. The leave did indeed provide the opportunity for second-tier leaders to develop their skills and abilities. "In some cases the sabbatical helped make clear to the organization that the person who acted as the interim executive director was the right choice," Linnell and Wolfred wrote in the study. "One group did a national search, but hired the deputy director who had acted as the interim because they had seen her leadership in action. Another organization had the opposite experience, where both the awardee and the interim mutually decided that the interim was not the right fit to succeed. The sabbatical process, in essence, allowed this organization to bench test a candidate for a new role."[20]

Taken together, the results of both studies mirror the experiences of companies that offer sabbatical programs. In addition to decreasing burnout and increasing engagement, sabbaticals are a surprisingly positive addition to leadership development and succession planning. All told, sabbaticals make for more and better company leaders. Experience and empirical evidence all suggest that the ROI on sabbaticals is significantly positive.

Mini-Sabbaticals and Paid-Paid Vacation

While months-long sabbaticals might still be hard for some companies to imagine, a few innovative leaders have experimented with reaping the same benefits of a paid leave but in shorter, more frequent increments. In essence, they've created mini-sabbatical programs. The Colorado-based contact management software company FullContact "bribes" its employees to take their full vacation time. They offer paid-paid vacation.

The program is the brainchild of company CEO Bart Lorang, who started the program in 2012. He has found it hugely beneficial. "It's an investment into the long-term happiness of our employees, which in turns leads to the sustained growth of our company," he said.[21] Under the program, FullContact gives employees $7,500 once a year if they take a vacation. During that time, they aren't allowed to work and must completely disconnect with the company.

Lorang believes that the policy ensures against what he calls the "misguided hero syndrome"—employees feeling that they need to be constantly connected and that without them the company would falter or break down. "It's almost like you have this adrenaline rush, brought on by the fact that people need you 24/7," he explained.[22]

These employees might work hard at first, but when the other areas of their lives begin to fall apart, they end up costing more value than they create. Lorang himself felt the damaging effects of misguided hero syndrome for several years, and it didn't turn out so well for him. After several failed relationships and a huge toll on his personal life, Lorang resolved to keep his employees—and himself—safe from the workaholic delusion. Lorang has been on several fully disconnected vacations himself since starting the policy.

The Motley Fool, a financial and investment advisement company, has run a traditional sabbatical program for some time. Under this program, employees earn four to six weeks of paid leave after ten years at the company. The company's leaders found the program so successful that they decided to create a miniature version to give similar benefits to less-vested employees. In their new experiment, which they call "the Fool's errand," one employee is randomly selected every month.[23] The winner must take a two-week-long vacation, fully disconnected from work, sometime in the month after winning. To incentivize winners to actually take the break, they also get $1,000 when they leave on vacation. Just as with the company's traditional sabbatical program, "the Fool's errand" also helps company leaders spot-check their organization and make sure that no department or project is too dependent on any one person.

According to Sam Cicotello, who oversaw the program during her time at Motley Fool, nearly half of the employees who "win" initially try to get out of taking the vacation, perhaps falling for misguided hero syndrome. "Almost everyone wants to win it until they win it," Cicotello said. Most do take the break eventually, and when they do, they get a chance not only to rest but to realize that the company will go on without them, furthering the chances that they'll disconnect more and more effectively in the future.

Mini-sabbaticals and personal downtime can have such a positive effect on reducing burnout, enhancing recruiting, and increasing performance that some entrepreneurs have experimented with moving them to the very beginning of an employee's tenure. Jason Freedman, founder and CEO of San Francisco–based 42Floors, a commercial real estate search engine website, instituted what he calls a "pre-cation."[24] Freedman said that the idea came to him while trying to recruit a new employee. "Every other company he was talking to was asking, 'How soon can you start?'" Freedman recalled. Freedman could see that the candidate was tired and beleaguered. Freedman wanted the guy, but not if he was burned out from the start.

So Freedman made him a job offer with an odd requirement. He had to take a two-week vacation before his first day. 42Floors would pay for the leave, and the new recruit could not start until he'd taken the vacation and recovered. Not only did Freedman get the new hire, but he got a much higher performer than other companies would have recruited. It worked so well that Freedman has since made it a mandate. All new employees are offered a job *and* a vacation. "The day they get their offer letter, it's kind of like Christmas morning," said Freedman. "It's like, 'Yeah, have a great time! And when you get back here, work your ass off!'"[25]

In the high-performance culture of the San Francisco technology industry, pre-cations may be the perfect mini-sabbatical to ensure that new recruits start with the company rested and ready to perform. Word of Freedman's idea quickly spread, and precations were soon imitated in other firms.

Atlassian, an enterprise software company with offices in Sydney and San Francisco, actually raised the bar. In addition to offering new hires some paid time off, the company also gives them a travel voucher and pushes them to take a trip before they arrive for their first day on the job. Jeff Diana, the chief people officer of Atlassian, said they started the program in 2010 as a new tactic in the war for talent that is recruiting, trying to spend less money on headhunters and more money on their future performers. "Changing jobs is an important shift, and we want to give people time to recharge, to spend some time with family," he said. "Because once you start a new job, you kind of jump all in."[26]

Another interesting twist on the mini-sabbatical can be found, appropriately, in the home office of TED, the very conference at which Stefan Sagmeister presented his experience in 2009. Like a lot of organizations, TED shuts down its offices between Christmas and New Year's Day. But the New York City nonprofit has also been shutting down every July for two weeks. The company gives a mini-sabbatical to *everyone every year.* "When you have a team of passionate, dedicated overachievers, you don't need to push them to work harder, you need to help them rest. By taking the same two weeks off, it makes sure everyone takes vacation," explained June Cohen, the executive producer of the TED conference.[27]

The organization made the shift in order to formalize a rest event that used to happen regularly. Originally, TED's only product was an annual conference. The entire year was spent planning the conference, and when the show was over everyone would take a break for a week before returning relaxed, refreshed, and ready to plan the next year. But after TED began posting talks from the conference online, the work schedule quickly evolved into a year-round endeavor. TED's leaders, perhaps after hearing Sagmeister sing the praises of the sabbatical, instituted the program to canonize what they had lost by changing their business model. "Planning a vacation is hard — most of us would feel a little guilty to take two weeks off if it weren't preplanned for us, and we'd be likely to cancel when something inevitably came up," said Cohen. "This creates an enforced rest period, which is so important for productivity and happiness."

Sabbatical, mini-sabbatical, pre-cation, mandatory vacation — all of these programs have one thing in common: they represent small investments that yield big returns. By giving employees structured time to rest and rejuvenate, new potential for creativity and high performance is unlocked. Where they all differ — in duration and structure — is a benefit for leaders looking to gain from giving leave. Each company experimented with a way to get the benefits of rest in a way that didn't disrupt its business model. For many companies, it was a formal sabbatical program, while for others it was smaller but more frequent leaves. Regardless, the positive returns experienced by all of these companies far outweigh the costs, and the empirical research backs up their experiences. Time away from work makes work better.

12

■

FIRE THE MANAGERS

Some of the most successful companies have opted to fire all their managers. Others have found ways to push some of the management function down to the level of those who are being managed. Research suggests that employees are most productive and engaged when they, and not their manager, control their destiny.

E MPLOYEES AT VALVE SOFTWARE don't have to take orders from "the boss."

That's because, at the Bellevue, Washington–based company, there are no bosses to give orders.

In effect, Valve is a company with no managers. They don't believe in managers, and they don't believe in job descriptions. When new people join the company, they rotate around on various projects, talk to lots of people, and then decide which project (or projects, if they decide to contribute to multiple areas) to jump into full-time.

"My observation is that it takes new hires about six months before they fully accept that no one is going to tell them what to do, that no manager is going to give them a review, that there is no such thing as a promotion or a job title or even a fixed role," wrote Valve employee Michael Abrash on the company's blog. "That it is their responsibility, and theirs alone, to allocate the most valuable resource in the company — their time — by figuring out what it is that they can do that is most valuable for the company, and then to go do it."[1]

Valve isn't just a small handful of programmers working in a garage either. The company was founded in 1996 by Mike Harrington and Gabe Newell.[2] Both were former Microsoft employees who decided to partner together; they actually signed the corporate paperwork the same day Newell got married. The company grew organically and quickly based on the success of its critically acclaimed game series *Half-Life*. The six-game series made a significant impact on the industry and won more than fifty game-of-the-year awards.[3]

That success was followed up by several other successful franchises and the release of Steam, an online distribution portal for video games — sort of an iTunes for video games that accounts for an estimated 70 percent of all video game sales worldwide.[4] Although the company is privately held, it's estimated to be valued at between $3 billion and $4 billion. The company has grown dramatically from the original partnership to more than 400 people.

Ordinarily, that type of growth would require that a fairly rigid hierarchy be put in place to manage everyone and keep them working in the right direction. But Harrington and Newell don't see it that way. "We thought about what the company needed to be good at," Newell said. "We realized that here, our job was to create things that hadn't existed before. Managers are good at institutionalizing procedures, but in our line of work, that's not always good."[5]

So Harrington and Newell chose to ignore the traditional structure and to build something new that would allow innovative and
talented people to thrive. While they often refer to this structure
as flat, it's really an ever-changing structure of various-sized teams
all working on whatever they deem to be the most important thing
to focus on. According to Valve's employee handbook:

> When you're an entertainment company that's spent the last de-
> cade going out of its way to recruit the most intelligent, innova-
> tive, talented people on Earth, telling them to sit at a desk and
> do what they're told obliterates 99 percent of their value. We
> want innovators, and that means maintaining an environment
> where they'll flourish.[6]

In fact, what Valve employees work on changes so much each
day that every employee's desk is equipped with wheels and organized such that only two cords need to be unplugged before it can
be rolled to wherever it's needed in the shop. "The mobility within
the corporation is a great asset, and everybody recognizes that,"
said Yanis Varoufakis, an economist from the University of Athens
who used to work as Valve's economist-in-residence.[7] Varoufakis
echoed Abrash's comment that it can take some time for new hires
to adjust. The culture is not for everyone. "It is a bit disconcerting
for people who enter Valve, because there is no one there to tell
them what to do."[8]

There are lots of people, however, to tell them what they *could*
do. Since Valve has no managers, all projects are started by an individual employee or a group pitching an idea to the company and
then recruiting a team. If enough people wheel their desks into
the group, the project starts. Sometimes an individual employee
is referred to as the "leader" for a project, but everyone inside the
company knows that this simply means that this is the person

keeping track of all of the information and organizing what is being done — not the person giving orders on what to do.

There are also lots of people to tell employees *how* they're doing. Valve may not have managers, but it does have a performance management system in place. Just like the work itself, the system works on a peer basis. A designated set of employees interview everyone in the company and ask who they've worked with since the last peer review session. They ask about their experiences working with each person. That feedback is collected and anonymized, and then every employee is given a report on their peers' experiences working with them.

A similar, but separate, system is also used to determine compensation. Each project group is asked to rank the members of the group based on four factors: skill level, productivity, group contribution, and product contribution. Once all that information is collected, Valve applies a series of calculations that place each employee in a compensation bracket.

Valve also empowers all of its employees to make hiring decisions, which it describes as "the most important thing in the universe."[9] Valve attributes the success of its organizational design to the fact that it hires the smartest, most innovative, and most talented people it can find. Making sure that it continues to hire only high-caliber people is vital to keeping the system working. The company's handbook reminds employees, "Any time you interview a potential hire, you need to ask yourself not only if they're talented or collaborative but also if they're capable of literally running this company, because they will be."[10]

Valve's success without managers or hierarchy can seem like an outlier compared to the norm at most organizations. However, their organizational structure is not necessarily a new or untried trend. As the nature of work has shifted, so have the means to keep that work organized and productive. Traditionally, the work of a manager entailed planning, organizing, commanding, controlling, reporting, and measuring. With the shift in the nature of work, other companies like Valve have found it beneficial to do away with the traditional management structure and allow employees to take control of many of these activities — to manage themselves, or at least shape how they are managed. Alongside the rising trend of managerless companies is a rising tide of psychological research that offers clues as to why nonmanaged workers often manage to work better.

The Origins of Autonomy

For several decades, two researchers have been at the core of trying to discover what drives human motivation, particularly what produces intrinsic motivation (the drive to engage in behaviors not because of external rewards but because of internal desire). Edward Deci and Richard Ryan, both professors at the University of Rochester, began their research in the 1970s by looking into motivation and its root causes. Their work would later be codified as "self-determination theory" and be expounded upon by legions of scholars around the world.

A fundamental tenet of self-determination theory is that one of the primary drivers of intrinsic motivation is autonomy, the universal urge to control choices in our lives and work. In fact, as their research progressed, Deci and Ryan began to see the challenge of intrinsic versus extrinsic motivation as really a matter of autonomous motivation versus controlled motivation.[11] "Autonomous motivation involves behaving with a full sense of volition and choice, whereas controlled motivation involves behaving with the experience of pressure and demand toward specific outcomes that comes from forces perceived to be external to the self," they wrote.[12]

In one study, Deci and Ryan (along with Paul Baard of Fordham University) studied frontline employees at a major American investment bank. For the study, 528 employees attended a departmental meeting where they were given a packet of questionnaires designed to measure a variety of constructs, including perceived autonomy support, which was a measure of how much their bosses considered their point of view, gave useful feedback, and provided them with choice over what to do and how to do it. The surveyed employees were also asked to submit their most recent performance evaluation. The researchers found a significant correlation between employees' perceptions of autonomy and their overall performance. In short, the more managers cede control over what to do and how to do it, the more employees do it well.

Building off of Deci and Ryan's work, the research has proven the benefits of autonomy all over the world, whether in the kind of knowledge work that goes on at Valve or in industrial work like manufacturing. In one study of working conditions and management practices in Nike's manufacturing plants, a team of researchers led by Richard Locke compared two identical T-shirt factories in Mexico. The two plants had virtually everything in common, from the products they produced to their economic, social, and political environments to the level of union presence in each plant. What differed between the two plants was the level of autonomy given to factory workers. In Plant A, workers were given freedom to organize themselves into teams, create work schedules, plan production targets, and divide up the various tasks. In Plant B, the workers were controlled and managed much more strictly, with production schedules and roles dictated by management. Locke and his team found that Plant A was almost twice as productive as Plant B, creating an average of 150 shirts per day versus Plant B's

80. In addition, Plant A produced those shirts at 40 percent lower cost, despite paying higher wages.[13]

Across the Atlantic, researchers in the United Kingdom led by Kamal Birdi of the University of Sheffield studied 308 manufacturing companies over an astoundingly long period — twenty-two years — and found that autonomy made a huge difference in productivity. The researchers tracked a variety of productivity-driving programs such as employee empowerment, supply chain partnering, total quality management, and just-in-time production. Over the more than two decades, the researchers watched as more and more plants adopted these management practices. In the end, very few of them had an isolated effect on performance. Only when companies adopted practices that gave employees autonomy (such as empowerment or team-based working) was performance improved. In the end, autonomy-related policies yielded a 9 percent increase in total value added per employee.[14]

Muammer Ozer at City University of Hong Kong found that not only does autonomy positively affect employees' performance, but it can also make them more loyal and responsible members of the organization. Ozer collected surveys from 266 jewelry workers and also from a coworker of each respondent and the immediate supervisor. The workers answered questions designed to measure the extent to which they had control over their jobs and also the extent to which they were willing to engage in routine organizational citizenship behaviors, such as helping their coworkers or offering ideas to improve the company's performance. Coworkers were asked questions about the strength of their relationship with the surveyed workers, and supervisors were asked to rate their performance. After he collected and analyzed all of the data, Ozer found that autonomy significantly influenced the workers' willingness to be good organizational citizens and also increased the strength of team relationships. That in turn had a significantly positive effect on job performance. In short, more autonomous individuals are better citizens, better friends, and better performers.[15]

This relationship finding is an important one, since autonomy isn't the same thing as independence. Autonomy is about having control over how you work, but it doesn't automatically mean that you work alone. "Autonomy means to act volitionally, with a sense of choice," write Deci and Ryan. "Whereas independence means to function alone and not rely on others."[16] Thus, it's possible to be autonomous but also interdependent with coworkers, relying on their work to support your own effort. In fact, the desire for autonomy (unlike the desire for individualism) appears to be a universal concept and not a cultural one. Researchers have validated the relationships between autonomy, well-being, and performance everywhere from the United States to Russia and Turkey to South Korea and Bangladesh.[17]

Autonomy also isn't the same thing as anarchy. In the workplace, it's about giving responsible freedom to employees, but different companies experiment with different levels of giving up control. Some industries and organizations find that they can't become totally managerless but they can in fact give some level of control back to individuals that might seem strange at first. "A financial analyst once asked me if I was afraid of losing control of our organization," wrote Herb Kelleher, the former CEO of Southwest Airlines, describing an objection to how employees are empowered to solve a variety of customer issues without needing to consult policy books or supervisors. "I told him I've never had control and never wanted it. If you create an environment where the people truly participate, you don't need control."[18] Kelleher's words echo the experience of Valve's leaders and corroborate the decades of research into the power of autonomy. No matter how many or how few managers you have on staff, if your staff doesn't feel that they can control their own work, their work will suffer.

"Managerless" Means Everyone Is a Manager

Valve isn't the only software company to experiment with a managerless structure. Shortly after its inception, the writing platform Medium adopted a self-managing structure to fuel its growth. Instead of a purely flat structure like Valve's leaders have put into practice, Medium is organized by self-managed teams, or circles of individuals, working on various projects.[19]

For example, there is a circle that tackles issues related to how users find and read content (the "Reading and Discovery" circle) and another focused on how content is created (the "Creation and Feedback" circle). Every circle or team has a dedicated purpose that contributes to the broader purpose of the company, but every circle is empowered to shape the project in any way that will fulfill the purpose. If a project gets too large for the team, they recruit another person internally or hire someone new. Hiring decisions, like all decisions, are made by individuals and teams and don't require management approval; there are no managers.

Flat hierarchies or self-managing structures are a growing trend in the software and technology world, where the product grows from the minds of the employees. But what about more traditional companies, where the product is built from raw materials or grows from the ground?

For over forty years, Morning Star Company has been doing just that.[20] Morning Star is the largest tomato processor in the world, handling almost one-third of the tomatoes processed in the United States every year. Founded by Chris Rufer in 1970 as a trucking operation, the company has grown to one that moves over 2 million tons of tomatoes each year, all under the power of autonomous, managerless employees. While Rufer remains the company's president, he doesn't give orders. Instead, all employees are responsible for writing their own mission statement, a short statement of how they will contribute to the company's mission of "producing tomato products and services which consistently achieve the quality and service expectations of our customers."[21]

Once that mission statement is drawn up, employees negotiate with every associate who will be affected by their role, and together they draw up a Colleague Letter of Understanding (CLOU). The CLOUs, some 3,000 of them, are renegotiated and rewritten annually. They're flexible, but they are, in essence, the organizational chart of the company. "The CLOUs create the structure," said Rufer. "This is spontaneous order, and it gives you more fluidity."[22] Morning Star's individual business units also negotiate CLOU-like agreements with all customers and suppliers. The belief is that CLOUs provide a better system for management performance than managers, since agreements reached by individual entities do a better job of aligning objectives and incentives than managers would. "If people are free, they will be drawn to what they really like as opposed to being pushed toward what they have been told to like," said Rufer.[23]

With agreements in place, employees are free to pursue their mission and objectives as they see fit. There is no purchasing department to approve equipment requests. If employees need something, they simply buy it. There is no human resource manager to decide when to hire new people. If colleagues feel like they are overloaded, they hire a new person to help get the work done.

While everyone is free to spend company resources, everyone is also accountable to the entire company for how those resources are spent.

All employees must consult affected colleagues and build a case for the return on investment. In addition, during the negotiation of CLOUs, employees draw up "stepping-stones" that serve as a means to track progress throughout the year. The company also publishes detailed financial reports twice a month that can be read by anyone. Still, there is no one person telling employees or divisions what budget to stay underneath and specifying the goals they have to hit. "I don't want anyone at Morning Star to feel they can't succeed because they don't have the right equipment or capable colleagues," said Rufer.[24] That success has been felt in a lot of ways. Rufer and his colleagues at Morning Star feel that their system allows for greater employee initiative and better judgment, while also increasing the expertise and collegial relationships among the employees. In the forty years since starting the company, Rufer has seen growth rates of ten times more than the industry average.[25]

Yet not every company that tries a managerless or self-managing structure has complete success. Total autonomy isn't for everyone. In 2015 Tony Hsieh announced that Zappos would be transforming its 1,500-person company into a fully self-managed organization.[26] Prior to the announcement, Hsieh had experimented with removing managers and empowering employees in certain areas of the company as a beta test for eventually rolling out a fully managerless design.

Recognizing that this plan might not be enthusiastically accepted by all employees (especially the managers who were about to be shifted back into individual contributor roles), Hsieh composed a long internal memo to employees to explain what they were doing and why they were doing it. The memo was also made public shortly afterward. In announcing the shift, the memo also revealed the details of a new form of "the offer" (see chapter 4). Hsieh said that if any employee in good standing studied the proposed format and decided that it wasn't for them and wanted to quit, Zappos would pay them three months' salary and benefits if they quit. "Self-management and self-organization is not for everyone, and not everyone will necessarily want to move forward," Hsieh wrote in the memo. He was right. Of the 210 people who quit, 20 were managers. Fourteen percent of the company decided that the new structure wasn't for them — a significantly higher percentage than for the new hires offered $4,000 to quit.

But that might not have been a bad thing. By building a 1,500-person company and then shifting its entire organizational design, Zappos was, in effect, asking everyone to work for a new company. Zappos's departing workers may have enjoyed the previous level of autonomy, but receiving that autonomy by removing all managers might have been an idea a bit too foreign to them.

Not every organization that benefits from maximizing autonomy can do so by removing all managers. At the General Electric aircraft-engine assembly facility in Durham, North Carolina, management still has a presence — a presence of one.[27] There is only one plant manager for the entire facility, and the hundreds of employees all report to that one manager.

More specifically, perhaps, all employees report to each other. Beyond the limited responsibilities of the plant manager, GE/Durham is a self-managed facility. Every aircraft engine is built by the team, and the team builds the production schedule. They receive one order from above: the date that a particular engine has to be ready for shipment. Beyond that, the team coordinates everything else — work schedules, task assignment, vacations, training, and team conflict.

The self-managed dynamic of GE/Durham's organization was a logical extension of a small idea. In 1993, when Robert Henderson was assigned the task of opening a new factory for General Electric, he happened on an unusual suggestion: what if every person who worked at the facility was required to be a licensed mechanic with the Federal Aviation Administration (FAA). "That would mean we'd start with a better caliber of employee, and we wouldn't have to spend time in fundamental training," Henderson said.

In a normal aircraft engine factory with an assembly line, not everyone needed to have an FAA license, and different people required different levels of management because of their varying skill sets. But if everyone started from the same high bar, then much less management structure would be needed and more could be handled by the team. The logical extension of this concept was that the assembly-line structure wasn't needed. So at GE/Durham one team builds all elements of the engine. One group handles every task in putting together a 10,000-part, 8.5-ton jet engine. They own that engine, and they take such good care of it that teams have even been known to jump onto the eighteen-wheelers that will deliver the engines and sweep out the truck beds so that no damage will occur in transit.

Everyone on the team is treated equally, and everyone knows what everyone else is paid. There are only three grades of technician based on skill set and only one wage for each grade. While the plant manager may be the only boss in the traditional organizational chart, the culture is such that everyone is accountable to the rest of their team. Everyone is everyone's boss. Larger decisions like human resources, safety policies, and processes are usually made by a council of elected members from each team.

As at Valve Software, hiring is a huge part of protecting the self-managed culture of GE/Durham. Beyond being FAA-licensed, new hires must be a cultural fit. Interviews can last eight hours, with five individuals interviewing each candidate, plus group activities designed to observe candidates in action.[28] Highly skilled individuals who don't seem capable of functioning in the team environment aren't given offers. This priority helps keep a strong team culture, which is also reflected in other ways. Everyone wears the same uniform. Tools and parts are left open and unguarded as a statement of trust, and team meetings happen every day. Each team works in two shifts, but in order to maintain everyone working the two shifts as one team, the shifts overlap so that every day at 2:30 p.m. all team members are together to share updates on progress, to troubleshoot together, and also to check in on morale, conflicts, and scheduling issues.

The results speak for themselves. On average, 75 percent of all engines shipped from GE/Durham are literally perfect. The remaining 25 percent usually have just a single flaw — a cosmetic scratch or a misaligned wire. That's a significant rate of perfection considering that designing and building an airplane engine is practically rocket science. Every bolt in the engine needs to be perfectly tightened with a torque wrench, and sometimes the room for error between parts is the width of a human hair.

Shortly after the plant opened, GE/Durham was able to maintain its high quality while reducing the cost of airplane engine assembly by 50 percent. Reflecting on the experience of designing GE/Durham, Henderson believes that the plant's success is less about having a manager or a certain number of managers and more about giving maximum autonomy. "We tend not to ask enough of people," he said. "People can do more than we give them credit for. We insist on maintaining tight control, but we really don't need to."[29]

In recent years, New Belgium Brewing has been experimenting with giving up that tight control. The Fort Collins, Colorado–based craft brewery has been turning ever more control over to its employees since its inception in 1991. Founded by Kim Jordon and her former husband Jeff Lebesch, New Belgium has grown to become the fourth-largest craft brewery in the United States and the eighth-largest brewer overall.[30] The company has developed a reputation for being a pioneer in alternative brewing and alternative management. Company leaders call it a "high involvement, ownership culture." And while traditional managers are still in the organizational chart, control and autonomy are pushed to all levels.

At the end of their first year at New Belgium, all employees are presented with a custom cruiser bicycle in front of the entire company. The bike itself is a symbol of the company's founding inspiration, a bicycle tour of Belgium taken in 1989 by Lebesch. That tour would be the influence for Fat Tire, the company's signature beer, and for Fat Tire's red bicycle logo. The custom bike comes with something else: *ownership.* All employees, owners or not, have access not only to the company's financial data but to financial literacy training that teaches them how to understand profit-and-loss statements, accounting ratios, cash flows — a vital piece of ownership since the company hires extremely diverse talent, everyone from microbiologists to carnival performers.[31] "I think people lose the power of feeling like an owner if they don't know what goes on behind the scenes," Jordon said.[32]

Ownership comes with decision-making power as well. Employees help shape the direction and big decisions of the company, often meeting to vote or achieve consensus before starting any new initiatives. In the late 1990s, the company had the opportunity to fulfill its goal of being environmentally sustainable by purchasing all of its power from a wind farm in Wyoming, but only if it could sign a ten-year contract and pay up-front. "We actually had that money in the bank, but we had already promised it to our co-workers as profit sharing," said Katie Wallace, the assistant director of sustainability at New Belgium.[33] So the entire company got together to discuss the issue, and after presenting the opportunity and the costs, the founders left the room. After just forty-five minutes of discussion, the group had reached consensus. They decided to forgo their profit-sharing checks and to invest the money in bringing wind power to the brewery.

New Belgium still uses a traditional managerial structure, but giving employees ownership and authority has been a way to reap the benefits of autonomy while maintaining a more traditional method of meeting the needs fulfilled by management. And this blend has worked so well that they've pushed it to the extreme. Recently, the company became 100 percent employee-owned, as Jordan sold her shares back to the employee stock ownership plan. (Lebesch left the business in 2001 and sold his shares back to New Belgium in 2009.) "When we made the announcement two years ago about whom we sold the company to, we gave each of our coworkers an envelope," said Jordon. "And inside the envelope was a mirror. That was our way of saying we sold the business to them."[34] Although not every employee has total control over the tasks of his or her job, all employees now have total control over the future of New Belgium.

The leaders of companies like Valve, Morning Star, and New Belgium experimented with different ways of providing autonomy to their employees, but all found the same power in giving up control. When individuals feel that they're free to determine what they're working on or how they work, they are more motivated, more loyal, and more productive. Decades of research support the individual anecdotes of these founders. To benefit from the motivating power of autonomy, leaders don't need to give up total control and fire all the managers, but every leader does need to consider how their current structure might be limiting the perception of freedom and blocking the organization from its peak potential.

13

■

CELEBRATE DEPARTURES

As individual job tenure in companies becomes shorter, leaders say good-bye to even their best people more frequently. How they do this — whether they celebrate or shun the departed — affects not just those leaving but those who stay, as well as the performance of both the old and new firms.

EVERY NEWLY HIRED consultant at McKinsey & Company thinks about quitting. In fact, most of the company's recruits think about their exit before they've even begun working at the firm. It's not really their fault either. Part of it is the nature of professional consulting. The firms that follow a partnership model are often referred to as "up or out" — either you get promoted through the ranks and make partner or you find your way out.

Every few years, McKinsey partners evaluate whether its consultants will move up the ranks; those deemed unlikely to move up are then gently pushed to leave the firm. Four out of five consultants at McKinsey don't make it to partner. They choose "out" either because "up" isn't an option or because it's no longer a desirable one. But the other reason new recruits think about leaving is that mentioning life after McKinsey is part of the recruiting process; it's part of life before McKinsey.

When recruiters for the firm visit business school campuses or meet with prospective applicants, they talk about the extensive impact of being McKinsey alumni. "We will talk about not just the great training you'll get and the great problems you'll work on and the wonderful clients you'll work with, but also the fact that the firm does celebrate those lifelong connections and how we keep our alumni connected," said Sean Brown, the global director of alumni relations at McKinsey & Company.[1] They mention that alumni from the firm have gone on to become CEOs of global companies, start entrepreneurial ventures, or transition into the nonprofit or government sector. All along the way, recruiters mention, McKinsey has been there to support its people. A page on the company's recruitment website plainly states: "As profoundly stimulating as it is at McKinsey, people do leave. We're OK with that. In fact, we're proud of what they achieve as global leaders . . . . We think it's great that there's a lot of McKinsey in places other than McKinsey."[2]

There's a lot to be proud of. In the company's more than nine decades of existence, the firm's consultants have influenced every major corporation on the globe and world leaders from a variety of countries. All of this impact comes from humble beginnings. McKinsey & Company began as the solo venture of James O. McKinsey in 1926.[3] McKinsey himself was an admirer and practitioner of Frederick Winslow Taylor's "scientific management" and originally positioned his consultants as "management engineers."

The firm continued to operate that way after James McKinsey's death in 1939 and up until 1950, when Marvin Bower took up the role of managing director for the firm. Bower is credited as the one responsible for transforming the firm's structure into one that would allow it to scale in geography and influence. It was Bower who changed the firm's consultants from management engineers to management professionals.[4]

Bower's approach was a bit different. For example, he insisted that all consultants wear fedoras — until President Kennedy abandoned the fashion. Bower forbade junior consultants from wearing argyle socks, thinking they would distract the firm's clients. It was Bower's mandate that every action should be designed to improve the image and the knowledge that the firm offered. It worked.

Much of the firm's impact ever since has stemmed from its ability to recruit new talent from the world's premier universities — including Rhodes scholars from Oxford and Baker scholars from Harvard Business School — and groom them into members of one of the world's prestigious sources of counsel.[5] However, McKinsey probably would not have traveled the path to prestige so easily without one distinctive company practice, the same one that new recruits might find so odd — *McKinsey celebrates departures.*

The first instance of celebrating departures happened during Bower's tenure. In 1957, a small group of former consultants organized a Christmas party in New York City. Although Bower forbade current consultants from attending, the firm did keep contact information for consultants who had left the firm and had sent them Christmas cards.[6] It wasn't long before this short list had become a full directory of the names of all former McKinsey consultants and was circulated inside and outside the firm as a means not only to allow current employees to stay in touch with old colleagues but also to let old colleagues stay connected to each other. Since then, the technology has been updated a lot, but the purpose has remained the same.

Today the hub for the McKinsey alumni network is a members-only website to which all alumni and current employees can gain access. The website features the directory of McKinsey alumni, sometimes including the home addresses and personal phone numbers of former alumni who now lead Fortune 500 companies. It also serves as the announcement center for McKinsey events. The firms hosts several knowledge events online and live events and conferences every year for alumni so that they can not only learn what McKinsey is up to but also gain information that they may need to stay competitive in their industry. "It's something that even the most senior alums get excited about because we're featuring content not just from our practices, but also from the McKinsey global institution," said Sean Brown.[7] Brown himself is technically a McKinsey alum as well as a current employee. He graduated from MIT's Sloan School of Management and joined McKinsey as a consultant for several years, then left to serve as MIT's alumni relations director. When McKinsey called him years later to see if he'd like to fill the same role for the firm, Brown returned to McKinsey to oversee the company's efforts to maintain a thriving network.

McKinsey's investment in maintaining the network is remarkable. In almost every one of its offices, the firm has at least one individual responsible for alumni engagement. The directory, the knowledge events, and the worldwide conferences are all funded by the firm. McKinsey sees this as a worthwhile investment, and not just for the reason you'd expect. McKinsey's alumni network does produce new clients for the firm, but that isn't the biggest payoff. "That's a very frequent assumption," said Brown. "In fact, we're much more focused on client impact and people impact."[8] The firm believes that by building a worldwide network of former consultants, it's better able to serve the needs of current clients. It's better equipped to recruit the best talent, but also better positioned to attain the knowledge needed to keep delivering outstanding service to clients. And there's a lot of evidence to support that belief.

Networks and Embeddedness

Companies that maintain alumni networks are in a better position to leverage a principle that sociologists call "embeddedness." Every industry is a network of connections: companies, clients, vendors, competitors, and partners. Embeddedness refers to a company's location in the larger network. And location matters: research shows that the strength of a company's relationships to other entities in the industry directly affects that company's financial strength.

This effect was first uncovered by Brian Uzzi (the same Brian Uzzi of the Broadway study) in research he conducted early in his career. In fact, it was his doctoral dissertation. Uzzi decided to study the garment industry in New York City, a complex network that he was already a little familiar with. "When my family came over here [the United States] from Italy, they all went into the needle trade. My grandfather was a tailor; my mother went to sewing school," he recalled.[9] Uzzi knew that the New York City garment industry was a network ripe for study, and he knew that different company leaders interacted differently. What he wanted to find out was whether their actions in the network made a difference for their company.

Uzzi studied twenty-three apparel firms in New York City and conducted interviews with each company's CEO and other key executives. In total, he collected 117 hours of interviews with forty-three people. He also observed interactions with company employees and distributors, customers, suppliers, and competitors. In addition, he gathered information on company transactions through the International Ladies' Garment Workers' Union (ILGWU), the trade union to which over 80 percent of New York's better apparel firms belonged. The union kept records on the volume of exchanges between different firms in the industry. Uzzi also modeled the likelihood of failure for each firm in the industry against his research on the companies, based on the number of firms that failed during the calendar year of his research. When he analyzed all of his research and compared a firm's network interactions with its likelihood of failure, Uzzi found something surprising.

As he suspected, different firms interacted in the industry differently, and the differences mattered. "Embedded networks of organizations achieve a certain competitive advantage over market arrangements," Uzzi wrote in his article on the research.[10] Some firms did business with only a few trusted vendors (what Uzzi labeled "close-knit ties"), while others portioned out their business by giving many small assignments to various firms ("arm's-length ties"). He found that having strong close-knit ties did increase a firm's chances of survival — but only to a point before being too close with too few firms began to have a negative impact.

The firms with the most success in the industry maintained a solid mix of close-knit and arm's-length ties and selectively chose which ties to use when. "There's this balance between having arm's-length ties that don't go as deeply into the relationship, but allow you to scan the market more broadly," Uzzi explained. "At the same time, the energy spent that you might put into a close-knit tie could have been split up among or across many arm's-length ties. That allows you to get information from many different points of view and then integrate it to produce the very best benefit."[11]

A firm that is too distant from all other firms in the industry can't leverage the benefits of trust or get help to solve the challenges they might face. At the same time, being too close to only a few other firms prevents the individual company from getting enough new market information and being adaptive to changes in the industry.

That balance between close-knit ties and arm's-length connections is exactly what a functional alumni network brings to its parent organization. Current employees and clients become the close-knit ties with whom the company interacts frequently. At the same time, former employees scattered across industries and sectors provide arm's-length ties that can relay important information and serve as important connections. "If I were running a company," Uzzi outlined, "I would want to maintain strong ties with some firms. But I would also like to have lots of looser ties that could be from my alumni network. Not necessarily people that I would want to approach and attempt to get new business from, but to use as more or less market research. So I could find out what's going on in their company, in their market — just kind of general information. I would want that mix of sources for market information."[12]

Sean Brown at McKinsey has found this to be true in his own experience. "I was on a health care study back when I was a consultant," he reflected. "We needed to quickly speak to health care executives at five different firms. It turned out we had alumni at all five of them. I called them up, and each one of them made time for me. I was just a two-year associate. They made time for me to talk about the issues that we were trying to figure out for our client."[13]

Brown has been on the giving end as well. "Fast-forward five years, I was now at the Sloan School, and I was contacted by another McKinsey study that was working with a university in Europe that was trying to start up their alumni program. I spent the time with them," he said. "I was busy, but I made the time for them because someone had done it for me in the past. You feel this connection to help maintain that network."[14] Sure, McKinsey generates new business from its former consultants who are running other firms, but more importantly, its alumni network serves as a critical connection to the broader network and fosters the optimal level of embeddedness that allows the firm to learn new information quickly, adapt swiftly, and stay competitive.

The Growth and Variety of Alumni Networks

Uzzi's findings make a strong case for competitiveness even in those industries that are far removed from consulting. Any company can benefit from using an alumni network to help maintain the right location in the broader network of its industry. Perhaps that's why corporate alumni networks are on the rise. According to one study, 67 percent of companies have had former employees organize alumni networks. And 15 percent of companies surveyed had formal alumni networks funded by the parent company.[15] In short, more and more companies are waking up and following the lead of companies like McKinsey by celebrating departures.

One strong advocate for celebrating departures is Reid Hoffman. Hoffman is the founder of LinkedIn, the place where alumni from various organizations self-organize their own networks. LinkedIn was several years old before anything like an alumni network was established, mostly owing to the fast growth of the company — the handful of alumni were simply outnumbered by brand-new employees and LinkedIn had to stay focused on new recruits.[16] As the company matured, however, the number of alumni grew, and the company's leaders knew the number of alumni would continue to grow.

Perhaps because they could see so many users of LinkedIn organizing informal alumni networks, Hoffman decided to act before the alumni ranks grew to an unmanageable size. "It became apparent that establishing a formal alumni network would be a good long-term investment," Hoffman explained.[17] The network

Hoffman and his team set up is fairly unique. LinkedIn's alumni network has two tiers. The first tier is all-inclusive: everyone who has ever worked with the company gains access to a special group on LinkedIn (the social network). Alumni are also given a lifetime premium membership to the social network, which ensures that they have an account (and also that they stay relatively familiar with the product).

Inside this group, current employees post updates about the company, including information originally found only in internal memos. A current employee also seeds the group's message board with questions and moderates the discussions that follow. The company circulates a quarterly newsletter to this group with not only information about LinkedIn but also news of notable alumni achievements and invitations to take surveys and provide intel that helps the company gain market information.

Entry into the second tier of the alumni network is by invitation only. Invitations are sent to the company's most valued alumni, either because of their past role in the company or because of their achievements post-employment (or their contributions to the first-tier alumni group). "This allows a manager to provide a higher level of service to loyal former stars in exchange for higher levels of engagement," Hoffman noted.[18] The invitations are sent directly from LinkedIn's executive leadership team. Having this distinguished first-tier alumni network allows for a deeper level of interaction between those alumni and the company's leaders. These alumni are even encouraged to participate in events back on campus at LinkedIn, everything from attending educational programs to judging company hackathons (short-term, collaborative sessions where programmers focus on new creative work). When the company held its initial public offering, Hoffman invited certain alumni to be part of the celebration and took time to celebrate their contribution to LinkedIn's big moment. Hoffman

even had bobblehead dolls of many early LinkedIn employees created — and by the time the company went public, many of these
original employees were alumni.

Because much of the information shared with alumni is repur-
posed from the company's internal memos and many of the alumni
programs are extensions of corporate events, the cost to LinkedIn
for maintaining its alumni network is minimal. But Hoffman believes that the return on investment is massive, whether it's in the
form of new candidate referrals or high-level market intelligence
that would cost hundreds of thousands if sought from outside analysts or consultants. The two-tier system allows the alumni network to combine LinkedIn's arm's-length and close-knit ties and
blends beautifully with the company's other network connections
to keep it located perfectly in its industry network.

Microsoft alumni unite not just to reconnect with each other
and with the company but also to make the world a better place.
For a long time, Microsoft alumni organized in two different
groups: the Microsoft Alumni Network, a more traditional alumni
program, offered a chance to reconnect with the company and get
access to special benefits, and the Microsoft Alumni Foundation
engaged former employees in philanthropy.[19]

Recently, the two groups joined forces to become one network
of more than 10,0000 former employees and gained even more
support from Microsoft's leadership.[20] Members of the network
actually pay a fee for joining. There are two levels of membership,
and joining gives members a variety of benefits, from employee
pricing at the company store and a free subscription to Microsoft
Office 365 (the company's core software product) to access to beta
programs and discounts on everything from insurance to travel
and dining.

In addition, their membership fees (and any additional dona-
tions) go to support various philanthropic causes, in some cases

ones started by other alumni. The Microsoft Alumni Network runs the "Integral Fellows" program, which awards grants to alumni who are directly engaged in nonprofit or philanthropic work. The network also organizes volunteer events for alumni and an annual reunion gala. Although the network operates separately from the company, it does so with Microsoft's blessing. Microsoft's senior leaders attend a lot of alumni events and are involved in supporting the governance of the network. In addition, Microsoft gives alumni access to the company's internal news portal, which allow alumni to stay as up-to-date on current events inside the company as they were when they were employed there. There's also an alumni directory with contact information for all former employees; like the directory McKinsey maintains, this database allows alumni to contact each other and allows the company to get in touch with an alum to share information.

The origins of Proctor & Gamble's alumni network are perhaps the most interesting. Recall from the discussion of noncompete clauses (chapter 6) that before A.G. Lafley led P&G, departed employees were in effect shunned by the company. "Up until 2000, when you left Proctor you were cut off," said Ed Tazzia, who was an executive at P&G for ten years and now serves as board chairman for the alumni network.[21] Shortly after Lafley assumed the reins of P&G and announced his intention to collaborate with outsiders to encourage innovation at the company, P&G alumni started gathering on their own.

In 2001, the Proctor & Gamble Alumni Network was formally started.[22] Now the network has chapters in dozens of cities worldwide. It also hosts two reunions a year, a global conference and an Asian regional conference—a testament to its global reach. The P&G Alumni Network is a nonprofit focused on keeping former employees connected and collaborating. Similar to Microsoft, one of the primary ways in which P&G alumni connect is through philanthropy. Also similar to Microsoft, the P&G Alumni Foundation operates underneath the larger network and raises money to award grants to various charitable causes.

The 25,000 members of the P&G Alumni Network have given over $700,000 to organizations that promote economic empowerment around the globe. Unlike their counterparts at Microsoft, the P&G Alumni Network also runs a speakers bureau that promotes former P&G employees as potential speakers at corporate events, industry conferences, and organizational meetings. The speakers all agree to donate their honorarium to the P&G Alumni Foundation. And the bureau's roster is stacked with some influential leaders: the network was able to identify over 130 former employees who went on to work as CEOs, presidents, or board members of large-scale companies, from Unilever to (coincidentally) Microsoft. The group even published a book in 2012, a collection of essays by alumni on how working at P&G set them up for future success.

Although the alumni network operates entirely independently from Proctor & Gamble, it operates with the company's support. P&G even granted the alumni network permission to use the company trademark as part of its brand. In addition, the network's website contains a page that gives alumni access to the Connect + Develop portal and allows them to continue to collaborate with their former employer.

The consulting firm Accenture boasts more than 100,000 alumni in the United States alone, mostly former consultants who, like McKinsey & Company alumni, stay connected to their old company through its online member portal and receive access to both a directory for alumni and a second directory of businesses started by alumni.[23] They also receive notifications about educational and social events for alumni and information about job opportunities, with a few unique twists. In addition to job openings at Accenture, the alumni network also encourages outside firms to post openings for which they're looking to hire former Accenture talent.

Perhaps most intriguing, the goal of soliciting these openings isn't just to find former Accenture people jobs at new firms, but also to help find the newest sources of talent for Accenture. The company actually offers Accenture alumni referral bonuses for suggesting candidates for Accenture job openings or even for general referrals for which there is a company fit.[24] Almost one-third of new hires at Accenture are candidates who were referred — and a significant portion of them were referred by former, not current, employees. Many companies offer bonuses when current employees find new employees, but Accenture is unique in offering its alumni bonuses for finding the next generation of future Accenture alumni. And the rewards are competitive with employee referral bonuses, ranging from $2,000 to over $7,000.

The bonuses provide a strong reason to stay engaged with the Accenture alumni network and job openings. In offering them, Accenture is unknowingly leveraging the power of the right mix of close-knit and arm's-length ties, not just to stay informed about the market but to stay informed about the market for people — a unique and successful strategy in the war for talent. Sometimes those posted job openings result in Accenture alumni becoming Accenture people once again. The company celebrates and welcomes back boomerang employees, but those boomerangs probably wouldn't be as willing to return without a thriving alumni network.

Finally, energy giant Chevron takes the concept of alumni networks and boomerang employees one step further. In addition to the standard corporate alumni network and online portal, the company also runs what it calls the "Chevron Bridges" program for contractors.[25] Bridges allows Chevron alumni to rejoin the company as contractors for technical assignments or as speakers, mentors, or advisers.

Most alumni are eligible for Bridges so long as they've been separated from the company for at least six months. Eligible alumni sign up via the alumni network website and are typically contacted for opportunities by one of the third-party contract agencies that Chevron works with. Chevron gets a discount from these agencies if alumni are hired, since the agency didn't have to work as hard to recruit those candidates. But that's not the only benefit Chevron gets. "The value and the knowledge they bring back is what we're really interested in," said D'Renda Syzdek, a former program manager for Bridges.[26] Syzdek's words echo the value proposition that Brian Uzzi found in studying the right mix of close-knit and arm's-length ties. In fact, the Chevron Bridges program actually predates the creation of the Chevron alumni network. Bridges was started around 2000, but didn't really take off until 2008, when it was plugged into the alumni network's online portal — further evidence of the value of alumni networks.

Companies that engage or build alumni networks are still in the minority, but their numbers are on the rise. As the nature of work and the nature of management change, the way even former workers are managed is changing along with it. The benefits that companies have reaped from networks, as well as the research on the importance of a proper blend of network connections, definitely support the concept of keeping in touch with former employees. Whether a company's efforts are as robust as the alumni networks of McKinsey & Company or Microsoft, any attempts to keep old employees connected and a part of the organizational network are likely to pay big dividends. There is real value in celebrating departures and making sure that a farewell simply becomes a "see you later."

Afterword:
Reinventing the Management Engine

As I was writing this book and collecting stories of companies and people who have abandoned the traditional thinking about management systems, I did, of course, encounter doubters. Not everyone is willing to concede that the success of these so-called radical practices suggests that our old tools have become ineffective.

I remember that one objection in particular seemed to keep popping up, voiced most often by people who'd spent the bulk of their careers inside the systems-favorable world of command-and-control management. "There's a reason these systems are traditions," the doubters would say. "They've been around a long time because they work."

Every time I encounter this kind of objection, my mind returns to the same analogy: the internal combustion engine. The internal combustion engine has been around a long time. As a system, it continues to power the majority of the cars driven around the world, as well as a host of other machines. It works, that's why it's still around.

But engineers and mechanics will tell you that the internal combustion engine is only about 25 or 30 percent effective.[1] When gasoline enters the engine and is ignited, some of the energy stored in the gasoline is used to push the pistons forward. But a significant amount of the energy is used to overcome inertia and friction, and some is used to pump air as well as the next stroke of gasoline into the chamber. In the end, only 30 percent of the potential energy given to the system is harnessed and channeled to achieve the goal of the overall system — the forward motion of the car.

The internal combustion engine works, and it's worked well for over 150 years. But that's only if you're willing to accept 30 percent energy-efficient as "working." True, as a system, it achieves the desired objective, but it does so while failing to capture a significant amount of potential energy. For much of the engine's history, we have had little choice but to accept this low threshold for efficiency. We couldn't design a better system, so we've defined the system we have as "working."

Over the years, the majority of improvements to the system — to the automobile — were about getting more movement out of that same 30 percent of energy. Fuel efficiency meant not how much energy was captured from the fuel, but how far a car could travel on the 30 percent of energy per gallon captured. Even the most cynical would have to agree that 30 percent is not especially efficient.

Yet some engineers never settled for this standard. Some innovators continued to experiment with the boundaries of the internal combustion system or explored new systems altogether. In their experimentation, some totally new engines have been created, while others are still being tinkered with. But each experiment reveals small clues that can lead to building a better (and more efficient) engine.

That 30 percent efficiency makes for a great analogy to organizations. Companies are charged with taking inputs of raw materials, capital, and human energy and then producing outputs that succeed in the marketplace. Organizations are the systems created to move from input to output, from resources and energy to profitability. When Frederick Winslow Taylor stepped inside the Bethlehem Iron Company, his goal was to get the most out of human energy that he could. His goal was to make the efforts — the energy — of the laborers as efficient as possible. For a time, the tools he developed did precisely that. Manufacturing output per labor-hour — the efficiency of the engine — increased significantly when Taylor's methods were applied. He didn't need laborers' minds; he was primarily interested in maximizing the efficiency of their bodies.

But when the world of work changed from industrial work to knowledge work, the *fuel* of the system changed too. Companies didn't need just the manual labor of their workforces to mass-produce standardized products. Instead, companies needed the mental energy of everyone on staff in order to solve problems and design whole new products. The fuel running most organizations today isn't brute labor — it's mental energy.

And overall, as a system for efficiently capturing mental energy, most organizations today are still working about as efficiently as the internal combustion engine. According to extensive and global research from the Gallup organization, only 13 percent of workers worldwide are engaged in their work.[2] In the United States, the number is somewhat higher, at around 30 percent.[3] "Engagement" represents how much mental and emotional commitment individuals make to the organization and its goals. Engaged employees care deeply about their work, their colleagues, and the mission of the organization. Engaged employees bring more of their mental energy every day to their work. It's not a perfect equivalent to engine efficiency, but it's not that far off. At 13 or 30 percent, companies are capturing only a minor amount of the mental energy that individuals could bring to the table. It's no surprise then that the organizations that engage a higher percentage of individuals experience greater profitability than their unengaging competitors.

When I interviewed Dane Atkinson, the CEO of SumAll who decided to share the amount of his and everyone else's salary with the whole company, he said something that continues to strike me as brilliant. It was an aside — he barely realized he'd said it — but it perfectly synthesized what all of these new managers and companies are doing by experimenting and striving to improve. We were discussing why it seemed like so many successful companies are departing from management as usual.

He said, "Great leaders don't innovate the product, they innovate the factory."[4]

Today's great leaders are the Frederick Winslow Taylors of the mental factory. Instead of considering how to build a system, or a company, that maximizes the brute force of laborers, they have focused on building a system in which individuals bring their whole selves to the work and the company captures a greater percentage of mental energy. When the nature of work shifts from industrial to knowledge-based, when companies need their employees to solve problems and design new products, then it becomes obvious that the new management system should put the employee at the center. Great leaders have focused on this obvious principle and reinvented the factory to maximize the desired efficiency. Under new management, these companies have found a better way to function more effectively. The people behind these counterintuitive ideas are factory-innovators: they are building a better engine. The result is a better company *and* better management.

The leadership practices and company policies profiled in this book are the result of experimentation in reinventing the factory — in effect, redesigning the engine. Yes, the old management traditions, the ones that have been around for a long time, still work. But they work about as well as the internal combustion engine. Great leaders don't settle for such low levels of efficiency. Instead, like Dane Atkinson, they experiment and innovate and find a better way.

Their new methods may seem counterintuitive — but they

shouldn't. Instead, these methods should be seen as what they are — honest attempts to build a better engine. They might not work, or might not work as well, inside every organization. But their success in their own companies should be seen as validation for leaders everywhere to start experimenting with their company. Their efforts may not work perfectly, but the old methods didn't work so perfectly either. If they can get efficiency, or engagement, up just a few percentage points, then it's clearly worthwhile to continue to experiment. If their people are moved to the center of their system and the rest of it is designed around them, then it's worth continuing to experiment. It's only through continued experimentation that we'll find a more efficient engine and a more engaging way to lead.

It's under new management that we can do better.

Next Steps

For further study about the new world of work, better management, and the research behind these new leadership practices, I've created a collection of extra resources, including full-length interviews with several leaders in this book, videos, recommended reading, and discussion guides. All of these resources are freely available at www.davidburkus.com/resources.

Acknowledgments

Every book is a team effort, and *Under New Management* has had an amazing team:

Rick Wolff, my editor, who saw the vision and helped bring it to reality, as well as Rosemary McGuinness, Taryn Roeder, Katrina Kruse, Bruce Nichols, and everyone at Houghton Mifflin Harcourt.

Giles Anderson, my agent, who talked me out of the bad ideas and into great ones.

Tom Neilssen, Les Tuerk, and all the folks at BrightSight Group.

Tim Grahl, Joseph Hinson, and Becky Robinson.

The large group of experts and leaders who made themselves available for interviews and informal chats: Liann Eden and Dena McCallum, Sean Brown, Lenny Mendonca, Andrew Dickson, Jelly Helm, Zac Carman, Dane Atkinson, Matt Mullenweg, Brian Uzzi, and Julian Birkinshaw.

The author friends who listened to my ideas and gave advice on both the book and getting it out in the world: Nilofer Merchant, Ron Friedman, Peter Sims, Ori Brafman, John Richard Bell, Tim Sanders, Todd Henry, Heidi Grant Halvorson, Mitch Joel, Joshua Wolf Shenk, and Tom Rath.

My research assistants, Jack Lucido and Rachel Guttman, and the entire faculty at Oral Roberts University, especially my close colleagues in the College of Business.

And perhaps most importantly, my wife Janna and our two boys Lincoln and Harrison, for letting me hide when writing beckoned and finding me quickly when it didn't.

Notes

Introduction: Management Needs New Management

1. Nikil Saval, *Cubed: A Secret History of the Workplace* (New York: Doubleday, 2014), 47.
2. Frederick Winslow Taylor, *The Principles of Scientific Management* (New York: Harper & Brothers, 1913), 69.
3. Thomas W. Malone, *The Future of Work: How the New Order of Business Will Shape Your Organization, Your Management Style, and Your Life* (Boston: Harvard Business Review Press, 2004).
4. Gary Hamel, with Bill Breen, *The Future of Management* (Boston: Harvard Business Review Press, 2007), 13.
5. Saval, *Cubed,* 52.
6. Ibid., 56.
7. Richard A. D'Aveni, "On Changing the Conversation: Tuck and the Field of Strategy," *Tuck Today* (Winter 2003), Tuck School of Business at Dartmouth, http://web.archive.org/web/20070804050415/http://www.tuck.dartmouth.edu/faculty/publications/voices_rad.html (accessed May 22, 2015).
8. William H. Whyte, *The Organization Man* (New York: Simon & Schuster, 1956).
9. See Irving Lester Janis, *Groupthink: Psychological Studies of Policy Decisions and Fiascoes,* 2nd ed. (Boston: Houghton Mifflin, 1982).
10. Patty McCord, "How Netflix Reinvented HR," *Harvard Business Review* 92, nos. 1–2 (2014): 74–75.
11. Julian Birkinshaw, personal communication with the author, May 26, 2015.
12. Hamel and Breen, *The Future of Management,* 13.

1. Outlaw Email

1. Sara Radicati, ed., "Email Statistics Report, 2014–2018," The Radicati Group (April 2014), http://www.radicati.com/wp/wp-content/uploads/2014/01/Email-Statistics-Report-2014-2018-Executive-Summary.pdf (accessed March 4, 2015).

2. "Atos Origin Sets Out Its Ambition to Be a Zero Email Company Within Three Years" (press release), Atos Global Newsroom, February 9, 2011, http://atos.net/en-us/home/we-are/news/press-release/2011/pr-2011_02_07_01.html (accessed March 2, 2015).

3. Thierry Breton, "Atos Boss Thierry Breton Defends His Internal Email Ban," BBC News, March 8, 2012, http://www.bbc.com/news/technology-16055310 (accessed March 2, 2015).

4. Paul Taylor, "Atos' 'Zero Email Initiative' Succeeding," *Financial Times,* March 7, 2013.

5. Andrew Cave, "Evernote Takes on Microsoft and Google," *The Telegraph,* May 26, 2015, http://www.telegraph.co.uk/finance/newsbysector/mediatechnologyandtelecoms/11629237/Evernote-takes-on-Microsoft-and-Google.html (accessed May 28, 2015).

6. Andrew Cave, "Why Silicon Valley Wants Email to Die," *Forbes,* May 26, 2015.

7. Rebecca Greenfield, "Inside the Company That Got Rid of Email," *Fast Company,* September 25, 2014, http://www.fastcompany.com/3035927/agendas/inside-the-company-that-got-rid-of-email (access May 28, 2015).

8. Radicati, "Email Statistics Report, 2014–2018."

9. Gloria J. Mark, Stephen Voida, and Armand V. Cardello, "'A Pace Not Dictated by Electrons: An Empirical Study of Work Without Email," in *Proceedings of the SIGCHI Conference on Human Factors in Computing Systems* (2012), 555–64, https://www.ics.uci.edu/~gmark/Home_page/Research_files/CHI%202012.pdf.

10. Ibid.

11. Lisa Evans, "You Aren't Imagining It: Email Is Making You More Stressed Out," *Fast Company,* September 24, 2014, http://www.fastcompany.com/3036061/the-future-of-work/you-arent-imagining-it-email-is-making-you-more-stressed-out (accessed March 4, 2015).

12. Shayne Hughes, "I Banned All Internal E-mails at My Company for a Week," *Forbes,* October 25, 2012.

13. Ibid.

14. Evans, "You Aren't Imagining It."

15. Kostadin Kushlev and Elizabeth W. Dunn, "Checking Email Less Frequently Reduces Stress," *Computers in Human Behavior* 43 (2014): 220–28.

16. Stephanie Vozza, "The Science Behind Why Constantly Checking Your Email Is Making You Crazy," *Fast Company,* January 6, 2015, http://www.fastcompany.com/3040361/work-smart/the-science-behind-why-constantly-checking-your-email-is-making-you-crazy (accessed March 5, 2015).

17. Michael Austin, "Texting While Driving: How Dangerous Is It?" *Car and Driver,* June 2009.

18. Vozza, "The Science Behind Why Constantly Checking Your Email Is Making You Crazy."

19. Tom de Castella, "Could Work Emails Be Banned After 6pm?" *BBC News,* April 10, 2014, http://www.bbc.com/news/magazine-26958079 (accessed March 5, 2015).

20. "Living Offline: Minister Halts After-Hours Contact for Staff," *Der Spiegel,* August 30, 2013.

21. S.P., "France's 6pm E-mail Ban: Not What It Seemed," *The Economist,* April 14, 2014.

22. Megan Gibson, "Here's a Radical Way to End Vacation Email Overload," *Time,* August 15, 2014.

23. Marcus Butts, William J. Becker, and Wendy R. Boswell, "Hot Buttons and Time Sinks: The Effects of Electronic Communications During Nonwork Time on Emotions and Work-Nonwork Conflict," *Academy of Management Journal* 59, no. 3 (2015): 763–88.

24. University of Texas at Arlington, "Employees Become Angry When Receiving After-Hours Email, Texts," *ScienceDaily,* February 27, 2015, www.science daily.com/releases/2015/02/150227131010.htm (accessed March 9, 2015).

2. Put Customers Second

1. Vineet Nayar, *HCL Technologies: Employee First, Customers Second* (Boston: Harvard Business Review Press, 2010).

2. Ibid., 36.

3. Ibid.

4. Ibid., 115.

5. Vineet Nayar, "How I Did It: A Maverick CEO Explains How He Persuaded His Team to Leap into the Future," *Harvard Business Review* 88, no. 6 (2010): 112.

6. HCL Technologies Ltd., *2013–2014 Annual Report,* http://www.bseindia .com/bseplus/AnnualReport/532281/5322810614.pdf (accessed February 18, 2015).

7. James L. Heskett, W. Earl Sasser Jr., and Leonard A. Schlesinger, *The Service-Profit Chain: How Leading Companies Link Profit and Growth to Loyalty, Satisfaction, and Value* (New York: Free Press, 1997).

8. Frederick F. Reichheld, and W. Earl Sasser Jr. "Zero Defections: Quality Comes to Services," *Harvard Business Review* 68, no. 5 (1990): 105–11.

9. Steven Brown and Son K. Lam, "A Meta-analysis of Relationships Linking Employee Satisfaction to Customers' Responses," *Journal of Retailing* 84, no. 3 (2008): 243–55.

10. Richard G. Netemeyer, James G. Maxham III, and Donald R. Lichtenstein, "Store Manager Performance and Satisfaction: Effects on Store Employee Performance and Satisfaction, Store Customer Satisfaction, and Store Customer Spending Growth," *Journal of Applied Psychology* 95, no. 3 (2010): 530.

11. Souha R. Ezzedeen, Christina M. Hyde, and Kiana R. Laurin, "Is Strategic Human Resource Management Socially Responsible? The Case of Wegmans Food Markets, Inc.," *Employee Responsibilities and Rights Journal* 18 (2010): 295–307.

12. S. Regani and S. George, *Employees First, Customers Second: Wegmans' Work Culture* (Hyderabad, India: ICMR Center for Management Research, 2007).

13. David Rohde, "The Anti-Walmart: The Secret Sauce of Wegmans Is People," *The Atlantic,* March 22, 2012.

14. Regani and George, *Employees First, Customers Second.*

15. Rhode, "The Anti-Walmart."

16. Regani and George, *Employees First, Customers Second.*

17. Danny Meyer, *Setting the Table: The Transforming Power of Hospitality in Business* (New York: HarperPerennial, 2006), 240.

18. Ibid., 238.

19. Hayley Peterson, "The Amazing Reward All Shake Shack Employees Got Today," *BusinessInsider,* January 30, 2015, http://www.businessinsider.com the-amazing-reward-all-shake-shack-employees-got-today-2015-1 (accessed May 26, 2015).

20. "Howard Schultz: Starbucks' First Mate," *Entrepreneur,* October 9, 2008, http://www.entrepreneur.com/article/197692 (accessed February 23, 2015).

21. Howard Schultz and Dori Jones Yang, *Pour Your Heart into It: How Starbucks Built a Company One Cup at a Time* (New York: Hyperion, 1999), 245.

22. Nancy F. Koehn, Kelly McNamara, Nora N. Khan, and Elizabeth Legris, *Starbucks Coffee Company: Transformation and Renewal* (Watertown, MA: Harvard Business Publishing, 2014).

23. Howard Schultz and J. Gordon, *Onward: How Starbucks Fought for Its Life Without Losing Its Soul* (New York: Rodale, 2011), 77.

24. Howard Schultz, "We Had to Own Our Mistakes," *Harvard Business Review* 88, nos. 7–8 (2010): 112.

25. Ibid., 113.

26. Koehn et al., *Starbucks Coffee Company.*

27. Starbucks Corporation, *Fiscal 2014 Annual Report,* http://investor.starbucks. com/phoenix.zhtml?c=99518&p=irol-reportsannual.

3. Lose the Standard Vacation Policy

1. Patty McCord, "How Netflix Reinvented HR," *Harvard Business Review* 92, nos. 1–2 (2014): 71–76.
2. Reed Hastings, "Netflix Culture: Freedom & Responsibility," *SlideShare,* August 1, 2009, http://www.slideshare.net/reed2001/culture-1798664 (accessed April 21, 2015).
3. McCord, "How Netflix Reinvented HR," 72.
4. Hastings, "Netflix Culture."
5. Ibid.
6. Netflix, "Starting Now at Netflix: Unlimited Maternity and Paternity Leave," August 4, 2014, http://blog.netflix.com/2015/08/starting-now-at-netflix-un limited.html.
7. McCord, "How Netflix Reinvented HR," 73.
8. Ibid., 72.
9. Hastings, "Netflix Culture."
10. Richard Branson, "Why We're Letting Virgin Staff Take as Much Holiday as They Want," *Virgin,* September 23, 2014, http://www.virgin.com/richard -branson/why-were-letting-virgin-staff-take-as-much-holiday-as-they -want (accessed April 21, 2015).
11. Zac Carman, personal communication with the author, April 22, 2015.
12. Dov Siedman, *HOW: Why HOW We Do Anything Means Everything* (Hoboken, NJ: Wiley, 2007).
13. Paul J. Zak, "Trust," *Journal of Financial Transformation* (2003): 17–24.
14. Ibid., 23.
15. Ibid., 24.
16. Jim Romenesko, "Tribune Publishing Rescinds Its Discretionary Time Off Policy," JimRomenesko.com, November 21, 2014, http://jimromenesko.com /2014/11/21/tribune-publishing-rescinds-its-discretionary-time-off-policy/ (accessed April 24, 2015).
17. Jim Romenesko, "Tribune Publishing Implements Discretionary Time Off (DTO) Policy for Salaried Employees," JimRomenesko.com, November 14, 2014, http://jimromenesko.com/2014/11/14/tribune-publishing-implements -discretionary-time-off-policy/ (accessed April 24, 2015).
18. Kevin Roderick, "Huge Change: No More Set Vacation or Sick Days at *LA*

Times," *LA Observed,* November 17, 2014, http://www.laobserved.com/ar chive/2014/11/tribune_unilaterally_elim.php (accessed 24, 2015).

19. David Musyj, "How One Hospital Is Recruiting and Retaining Top Talent," *HospitalNews,* January 18, 2015, http://hospitalnews.com/one-hospital-re cruiting-retaining-top-talent/ (accessed April 24, 2015).

20. Marla Tabaka, "Why Richard Branson Thinks Unlimited Vacation Time Is Awesome — And You Should, Too," *Inc.,* October 6, 2014, http://www.inc.com /marla-tabaka/richard-branson-s-unlimited-vacation-policy-will-it-work -for-your-business.html (accessed April 24, 2015).

21. Siedman, *How,* 71.

4. Pay People to Quit

1. Frances Frei and Anne Morriss, *Uncommon Service: How to Win by Putting Customers at the Core of Your Business* (Boston: Harvard Business Review Press, 2012).

2. Quoted in "The Upside of Quitting" (audio podcast, 2011), produced by Stephen J. Dubner, http://freakonomics.com/2011/09/30/new-freakonomics -radio-podcast-the-upside-of-quitting/ (accessed March 16, 2015).

3. Frances Frei, Robin J. Ely, and Laura Winig, *Zappos.com 2009: Clothing, Customer Service, and Company Culture* (Boston: Harvard Business School Publishing, 2011).

4. Tony Hsieh, *Delivering Happiness: A Path to Profits, Passion, and Purpose* (New York: BusinessPlus, 2010), 47.

5. O. Y. Koo, *CASE: Zappos.com (Part B): Strategy Powered by Culture and People* (Blue Ocean Strategy Institute [INSEAD], 2013).

6. Hsieh, *Delivering Happiness,* 47.

7. Frei et al., *Zappos.com 2009,* 5.

8. Ibid.

9. Frei and Morriss, *Uncommon Service.*

10. Ibid.

11. Hal R. Arkes and Catherine Blumer, "The Psychology of Sunk Cost," *Organizational Behavior and Human Decision Processes* 35 (1985): 124–40.

12. Ibid., 126.

13. Gallup, *State of the American Workplace: Employee Engagement Insights for US Business Leaders,* 2013, http://employeeengagement.com/wp-content /uploads/2013/06/Gallup-2013-State-of-the-American-Workplace-Report .pdf.

14. Leon Festinger, *When Prophecy Fails: A Social and Psychological Study of*

a Modern Group That Predicted the Destruction of the World (New York: Harper-Torchbooks, 1956).

15. Jack Brehm, "Post-Decision Changes in Desirability of Alternatives," *Journal of Abnormal and Social Psychology* 52, no. 3 (1956): 384–89.

16. Quoted in Dubner, *The Upside of Quitting.*

17. Gallup, *State of the American Workplace.*

18. Jeff Bezos, "Annual Letter to Shareholders," 2013, file:///C:/Users/Cynthia%20Buck/Downloads/2013%20Letter%20to%20Shareholders.pdf.

19. Ibid.

20. Bill Taylor, "Why Amazon Is Copying Zappos and Paying Employees to Quit," *Harvard Business Review,* April 21, 2014 .

21. Gallup, *State of the American Workplace.*

22. Riot Games, "Announcing Queue Dodge," June 19, 2014, http://www.riotgames.com/articles/20140619/1304/announcing-queue-dodge (accessed March 17, 2014).

5. Make Salaries Transparent

1. Dane Atkinson, personal communication with the author, February 26, 2015.

2. Ibid.

3. HRNext.com Survey, discussed in Peter Bamberger and Elena Belogolovsky, "The Impact of Pay Secrecy on Individual Task Performance," *Personnel Psychology* 63 (2010): 965–96.

4. F. Steele, *The Open Organization: The Impact of Secrecy and Disclosure on People and Organizations* (Reading, MA: Addison-Wesley, 1975).

5. Royal Swedish Academy of Sciences, Nobel Foundation, "The Sveriges Riksbank Prize in Economic Sciences in Memory of Alfred Nobel 2001: Information for the Public" (press release), Nobelprize.org, October 10, 2001, http://www.nobelprize.org/nobel_prizes/economic-sciences/laureates/2001/press.html (accessed September 16, 2014).

6. Atkinson, personal communication, February 26, 2015.

7. Rachel Emma Silverman, "Psst . . . This Is What Your Co-worker Is Paid," *Wall Street Journal,* January 29, 2013.

8. Atkinson, personal communication, February 26, 2015.

9. Ibid.

10. Sean Blanda, "Breaking Workplace Taboos: A Conversation About Salary Transparency," 99U, http://99u.com/articles/15527/the-age-of-salary-transparency (accessed September 15, 2014).

11. Joel Gascoigne, "Introducing Open Salaries at Buffer: Our Transparent For-

mula and All Individual Salaries," BufferOpen, December 19, 2013, http://
open.bufferapp.com/introducing-open-salaries-at-buffer-including-our
-transparent-formula-and-all-individual-salaries/ (accessed September 24,
2014).

12. Ibid.
13. Blanda, "Breaking Workplace Taboos."
14. Gascoigne, "Introducing Open Salaries at Buffer."
15. Ibid.
16. Vickie Elmer, "After Disclosing Employee Salaries, Buffer Was Inundated
with Resumes," *Quartz,* January 24, 2014, http://qz.com/169147/applications
-have-doubled-to-the-company-that-discloses-its-salaries/ (accessed September 24, 2014).
17. Alison Griswold, "Here's Why Whole Foods Lets Employees Look Up Each
Other's Salaries," *Business Insider,* March 3, 2014, http://www.businessinsider
.com/whole-foods-employees-have-open-salaries-2014-3 (accessed September 25, 2014).
18. Charles Fishman, "Whole Foods Is All Teams," *Fast Company,* April–May1996,
http://www.fastcompany.com/26671/whole-foods-all-teams (accessed February 5, 2015).
19. Elena Belogolovsky and Peter Bamberger, "Signaling in Secret: Pay for Performance and the Incentive and Sorting Effects of Pay Secrecy," *Academy of
Management Journal* 57, no. 6 (2014): 1706–33.
20. Emiliano Huet-Vaughn, "Striving for Status: A Field Experiment on Relative
Earnings and Labor Supply," working paper (Berkeley: University of California, November 2013), http://econgrads.berkeley.edu/emilianohuet-vaughn
/files/2012/11/JMP_e.pdf (accessed September 25, 2014).
21. John Stacey Adams, "Inequity in Social Exchange," in *Advances in Experimental Social Psychology,* vol. 2, edited by Leonard Berkowitz, 267–99 (New
York: Academic Press, 1965).
22. Bamberger and Belogolovsky, "The Impact of Pay Secrecy."
23. Edward E. Lawler III, "Pay Secrecy: Why Bother?" *Forbes,* September 12,
2012.
24. Gary R. Siniscalco, "Developments in Equal Pay Law: The Lilly Ledbetter Act and Beyond," ABA National Conference on Equal Employment Law (March 2010), http://www.americanbar.org/content/dam/aba
/administrative/labor_law/meetings/2010/2010_eeo_007.authcheckdam
.pdf.
25. Gowri Ramachandran, "Pay Transparency," *Penn State Law Review* 116, no.
4 (2012): 1043–80.

26. Ariane Hegewisch et al., "Pay Secrecy and Wage Discrimination 3," Fact Sheet C382, June 2011 (Washington, DC: Institute for Women's Policy Research).

27. David Card, Alexandre Mas, Enrico Moretti, and Emmanuel Saez, "Inequality at Work: The Effect of Peer Salaries on Job Satisfaction," working paper (November 2011), http://www.princeton.edu/~amas/papers/card-mas-moretti-saezAER11ucpay.

28. Alina Tugend, "Secrecy About Salaries May Be on the Wane," *New York Times,* August 22, 2014.

29. Atkinson, personal communication, February 26, 2015.

30. Ibid.

31. Fishman, "Whole Foods Is All Teams."

32. Elmer, "After Disclosing Employee Salaries."

6. Ban Noncompetes

1. *The Economist,* "Schumpeter: Ties That Bind," *The Economist,* December 14, 2013.

2. Steven Greenhouse, "Noncompete Clauses Increasingly Pop Up in Array of Jobs," *New York Times,* June 8, 2014.

3. Dave Jamieson, "Jimmy John's Makes Low-Wage Workers Sign 'Oppressive' Noncompete Agreements," *Huffington Post,* October 13, 2014, http://www.huffingtonpost.com/2014/10/13/jimmy-johns-non-compete_n_5978180.html (accessed March 24, 2015).

4. Ibid.

5. Dave Jamieson, "Jimmy John's 'Oppressive' Noncompete Agreement Survives Court Challenge," *Huffington Post,* April 10, 2015, http://www.huffingtonpost.com/2015/04/10/jimmy-johns-noncompete-agreement_n_7042112.html.

6. Warren Throckmorton, "Megachurch Methods: Pastor Fired Because He Wouldn't Sign Non-Compete Clause," *Patheos,* May 28, 2014, http://www.patheos.com/blogs/warrenthrockmorton/2014/05/28/megachurch-methods-pastor-fired-because-he-wouldnt-sign-non-compete-clause/ (accessed April 23, 2015).

7. Ibid.

8. Orly Lobel, *Talent Wants to Be Free: Why We Should Learn to Love Leaks, Raids, and Free Riding* (New Haven, CT: Yale University Press, 2013).

9. *The Economist,* "Schumpeter: Ties That Bind."

10. Lobel, *Talent Wants to Be Free.*

11. ABA Committee on Professional Ethics, formal opinion 61-300 (1961).

12. Lobel, *Talent Wants to Be Free.*

13. Ibid.

14. AnnaLee Saxenian, *Regional Advantage: Culture and Competition in Silicon Valley and Route 128* (Cambridge, MA: Harvard University Press, 1994).

15. Matt Marx, Jasjit Singh, and Lee Fleming, "Regional Disadvantage? Employee Non-compete Agreements and Brain Drain," *Research Policy* 44, no. 2 (2015): 394–404.

16. Carmen Nobel, "Non-competes Push Talent Away," Harvard Business School: Working Knowledge, July 11, 2011, http://hbswk.hbs.edu/item/6759 .html (accessed March 18, 2015).

17. Marx et al., "Regional Disadvantage."

18. Rafael A. Corredoira and Lori Rosenkopf, "Should Auld Acquaintance Be Forgot? The Reverse Transfer of Knowledge Through Mobility Ties," *Strategic Management Journal* 31, no. 2 (2010): 159–81.

19. On Amir and Orly Lobel, "How Noncompetes Stifle Performance," *Harvard Business Review* 92, nos. 1–2 (2014): 26.

20. Lobel, *Talent Wants to Be Free,* 177.

21. Sarah Jane Rothenfluch, "Dan Wieden Talks About W+K," *Think Out Loud* (Oregon Public Broadcasting), May 8, 2013, http://www.opb.org /radio/programs/thinkoutloud/segment/dan-wieden-talks-about-wk/ (accessed March 30, 2015).

22. Jelly Helm, personal communication with the author, June 3, 2015.

23. Lobel, *Talent Wants to Be Free.*

24. Lee Fleming and Koen Frenken, "The Evolution of Inventor Network in the Silicon Valley and Boston Regions," *Advances in Complex Systems* 10, no. 1 (2007): 53–71.

25. Lobel, *Talent Wants to Be Free.*

26. Ibid.

27. MLab, "Innovating Innovation: Proctor & Gamble," http://www.management lab.org/files/u2/pdf/case%20studies/procter.pdf (accessed April 1, 2015).

28. P&G, "Febreze® Embracing C+D to Become a Billion $ Brand," January 1, 2013, http://www.pgconnectdevelop.com/home/stories/cd-stories/20130101 -febreze-embracing-cd-to-become-a-billion-brand.html (accessed April 1, 2015).

29. Mike Addison, "P&G Connect and Develop — An Innovation Strategy That Is Here to Stay," Inside P&G, http://www.pg.com/en_UK/news-views /Inside_PG-Quarterly_Newsletter/issue2/innovation3.html (accessed April 1, 2015).

7. Ditch Performance Appraisals

1. Rebecca Hinds, Robert Sutton, and Hayagreeva Rao, "Adobe: Building Momentum by Abandoning Annual Performance Reviews for 'Check-ins,'" Stanford Graduate School of Business Case Study HR38, July 25, 2014, file:/// C:/Users/Cynthia%20Buck/Downloads/HR38.pdf.

2. Ibid., 1.

3. Ibid., 13.

4. Ibid.

5. Claire Suddath, "Performance Reviews: Why Bother?" *Bloomberg BusinessWeek,* November 7, 2013, http://www.bloomberg.com/bw/articles/20 13-11-07/the-annual-performance-review-worthless-corporate-ritual (accessed January 30, 2015).

6. Elton Mayo, "Hawthorne and the Western Electric Company," in *The Social Problems of an Industrial Civilization* (New York: Macmillan, 1933).

7. National Research Council, *Pay for Performance: Evaluating Performance Appraisal and Merit Pay* (Washington, DC: National Academies Press, 1991), 16.

8. Jack Welch and John A. Byrne, *Jack: Straight from the Gut* (New York: Business Plus, 2001).

9. Jacob Morgan, *The Future of Work: Attract New Talent, Build Better Leaders, and Create a Competitive Organization* (San Francisco: Jossey-Bass, 2014).

10. Leslie Kwoh, "'Rank and Yank' Retains Vocal Fans," *Wall Street Journal,* January 31, 2012.

11. Phyllis Korkki, "Invasion of the Annual Reviews," *New York Times,* November 23, 2013.

12. Don VandeWalle, "Development and Validation of a Work Domain Goal Orientation Instrument," *Educational and Psychological Measurement* 8 (1997): 995–1015.

13. Carol S. Dweck, *Mindset: The New Psychology of Success* (New York: Random House, 2006).

14. Satoris S. Culbertson, Jaime B. Henning, and Stephanie C. Payne, "Performance Appraisal Satisfaction: The Role of Feedback and Goal Orientation," *Journal of Personnel Psychology* 12, no. 4 (2013): 189–95.

15. Jena McGregor, "Study Finds That Basically Every Single Person Hates Performance Reviews," *Washington Post,* January 27, 2014.

16. Tom Warren, "Microsoft Axes Its Controversial Employee-Ranking System," *The Verge,* November 13, 2013, http://www.theverge.com/2013/11/12 /5094864/microsoft-kills-stack-ranking-internal-structure (accessed January 30, 2013).

17. Kurt Eichenwald, "Microsoft's Lost Decade," *Vanity Fair* 624 (2012): 108–35.
18. Warren, "Microsoft Axes Its Controversial Employee-Ranking System."
19. Tom DiDonato, "Stop Basing Pay on Performance Reviews," *Harvard Business Review,* January 10, 2014.
20. John Pletz, "The End of 'Valued Performers' at Motorola," *Crain's Chicago Business,* November 2, 2013, http://www.chicagobusiness.com/article/20131102/ISSUE01/311029980/the-end-of-valued-performers-at-motorola (accessed February 1, 2015).
21. Julie Cook Ramirez, "Rethinking the Review," Human Resource Executive Online, July 24, 2013, http://www.hreonline.com/HRE/view/story.jhtml?id=534355695 (accessed February 1, 2015).

8. Hire as a Team

1. Gary Hamel, *The Future of Management* (Boston: Harvard Business Review Press, 2007), 75.
2. Whole Foods Market, "Whole Foods Market History," http://www.wholefoodsmarket.com/company-info/whole-foods-market-history (accessed February 4, 2015).
3. Whole Foods Market, "Why We're a Great Place to Work," 2015, http://www.wholefoodsmarket.com/careers/why-were-great-place-work (accessed February 5, 2015).
4. John Mackey and Sisodia Rajendra, *Conscious Capitalism: Liberating the Heroic Spirit of Business* (Boston: Harvard Business Review Press, 2013).
5. CNN Money, "Whole Foods' Hiring Recipe" (video file), January 20, 2011, https://www.youtube.com/watch?v=ZLj9yuai7Q4 (accessed February 5, 2015).
6. Hamel, *The Future of Management.*
7. Peter F. Drucker, *On the Profession of Management* (Boston: Harvard Business School Press, 1998), ix–x.
8. Boris Groysberg, Ashish Nanda, and Nitin Nohria, "The Risky Business of Hiring Stars," *Harvard Business Review* 82, no. 5 (2004): 92–100.
9. Boris Groysberg and Linda-Eling Lee, "The Effect of Colleague Quality on Top Performance: The Case of Security Analysts," *Journal of Organizational Behavior* 29, no. 8 (2008): 1123–44.
10. Boris Groysberg, Linda-Eling Lee, and Robin Abrahams, "What It Takes to Make 'Star' Hires Pay Off," *Sloan Management Review* 51, no. 2 (2010): 57–61.
11. Matt Mullenweg, personal communication with the author, March 10, 2015.
12. Ibid.
13. Ibid.

14. Matt Mullenweg, "The CEO of Automattic on Holding 'Auditions' to Build a Strong Team," *Harvard Business Review* 92, no. 4 (2014): 42.
15. Mullenweg, personal communication, March 10, 2015.
16. J. J. Colao, "An Extended Interview with WordPress Creator Matt Mullenweg," *Forbes*, June 11, 2014.
17. Mullenweg, personal communication, March 10, 2015.
18. Laszlo Bock, *Work Rules: Insights from Inside Google That Will Transform How You Live and Lead* (New York: Twelve, 2015), 21.
19. Ibid., 105.
20. Business and Legal Reports, "Team-Based Hiring Approach Minimizes Turnover," in *Best Practices in Recruitment and Retention* (Old Saybrook, CT: Business and Legal Reports, 2006).

9. Write the Org Chart in Pencil

1. Heidi K. Gardner and Robert G. Eccles, *Eden McCallum: A Network-Based Consulting Firm* (Harvard Business School case study) (Watertown, MA: Harvard Business School Publishing, 2011).
2. Julian Birkinshaw, "Making the Firm Flexible," *Business Strategy Review* 18, no. 1 (2007): 62–87.
3. Liann Eden, personal communication with the author, February 5, 2015.
4. Freek Vermeulen, *Eden McCallum: Disrupting Management Consulting*, London Business School case study, 2014.
5. Eden, personal communication, February 5, 2015.
6. Birkinshaw, "Making the Firm Flexible."
7. Eden, personal communication, February 5, 2015.
8. Ibid.
9. Alfred D. Chandler Jr. *The Visible Hand: The Managerial Revolution in American Business* (Cambridge, MA: Harvard University Press, 1977).
10. Alexander Hamilton Institute, *Organization Charts* (New York: Alexander Hamilton Institute, 1923), 6.
11. Roger Martin, "Rethinking the Decision Factory," *Harvard Business Review* 91, no. 10 (2013): 96–104.
12. Ibid., 101.
13. Ibid.
14. Clayton M. Christensen, Dina Wang, and Derek van Bever, "Consulting on the Cusp of Disruption," *Harvard Business Review* 91, no. 10 (2013): 106–14.
15. Vermeulen, *Eden McCallum*.
16. Ibid., 2.

17. Eden, personal communication, February 5, 2015.
18. Brian Uzzi and Jarrett Spiro, "Collaboration and Creativity: The Small World Problem," *American Journal of Sociology* 111, no. 2 (2005): 447–504.
19. Brian Uzzi, interview with the author, March 11, 2014.
20. Uzzi and Spiro, "Collaboration and Creativity."
21. Uzzi, interview with the author, March 11, 2014.
22. Eden, personal communication, February 5, 2015.
23. Dane Atkinson, personal communication with the author, February 26, 2015.
24. Jeffrey Pfeffer and Robert I. Sutton, *Hard Facts, Dangerous Half-Truths, and Total Nonsense: Profiting from Evidence-Based Management* (Boston: Harvard Business School Press, 2006).
25. Tom Kelley, with Jonathan Littman, *The Art of Innovation: Lessons in Creativity from IDEO, America's Leading Design Firm* (New York: Currency, 1995).
26. Pfeffer and Sutton, *Hard Facts, Dangerous Half-Truths, and Total Nonsense,* 175.
27. Kelley and Littman, *The Art of Innovation.*
28. Teresa Amabile, Colin M. Fisher, and Juliana Pillemer, "IDEO's Culture of Helping," *Harvard Business Review* 92, nos. 1–2 (2014): 58.

10. Close Open Offices

1. David Dix, "Virtual Chiat," *Wired,* July 1994, http://archive.wired.com/wired/archive/2.07/chiat.html (accessed May 20, 2015).
2. Nikil Sival, *Cubed: A Secret History of the Workplace* (New York: Doubleday, 2014).
3. Maria Konnikova, "The Open-Office Trap," *The New Yorker,* January 7, 2014.
4. Michael Barbaro, "The Bullpen Bloomberg Built: Candidates Debate Its Future," *New York Times,* March 22, 2013.
5. Kevin Kruse, "Facebook Unveils New Campus: Will Workers Be Sick, Stressed, and Dissatisfied?" *Forbes,* August 25, 2012.
6. Karl Stark and Bill Stewart, "Open-Plan Office: An Introvert's Worse Nightmare," *Inc.,* February 28, 2013, http://www.inc.com/karl-and-bill/open-plan-office-an-introverts-worse-nightmare.html.
7. Aoife Brennan, Jasdeep S. Chugh, and Theresa Kline, "Traditional Versus Open Office Design: A Longitudinal Field Study," *Environment and Behavior* 34, no. 3 (2002): 279–99.
8. Jungsoo Kim and Richard de Dear, "Workspace Satisfaction: The Privacy-

Communication Trade-off in Open-Plan Offices," *Journal of Environmental Psychology* 36 (2013): 18–26.

9. Matthew C. Davis, Desmond J. Leach, and Chris W. Clegg, "The Physical Environment of the Office: Contemporary and Emerging Issues," in *International Review of Industrial and Organizational Psychology 2011,* vol. 26, edited by Gerard P. Hodgkinson and J. Kevin Ford (Chichester, UK: John Wiley & Sons, Ltd, 2011).

10. Gary W. Evans and Dana Johnson, "Stress and Open-Office Noise," *Journal of Applied Psychology* 85, no. 5 (2000): 779–83.

11. Jan H. Pejtersen, Helene Feveile, Karl B. Christensen, and Hermann Burr, "Sickness Absence Associated with Shared and Open-Plan Offices — A National Cross-sectional Questionnaire Survey," *Scandinavian Journal of Work, Environment, and Health* (2011): 376–82.

12. So Young Lee and Jay L. Brand, "Effects of Control over Office Workspace on Perceptions of the Work Environment and Work Outcomes," *Journal of Environmental Psychology* 25, no. 3 (2005): 323–33.

13. David Burkus, "0513: David Craig: The History of Workplace Design and Its Effect on Culture and Performance," LDRLB (podcast), June 23, 2014, http://davidburkus.com/2014/06/0513-david-craig/ (accessed May 20, 2015).

14. Keiko Morris, "More New York Companies Experiment with Innovative Office Space," *Wall Street Journal,* July 7, 2015.

15. Ibid.

16. Belinda Lanks, "Cozy in Your Cubicle? An Office Design Alternative May Improve Efficiency," *Bloomberg BusinessWeek,* September 18, 2014, http://www.bloomberg.com/bw/articles/2014-09-18/activity-based-working-office-design-for-better-efficiency (accessed May 20, 2015).

17. GLG, "GLG's New Global Headquarters Pioneers Latest Approach to Office Design and Culture" (video file), 2014, https://vimeo.com/100165888 (accessed May 20, 2015).

11. Take Sabbaticals

1. Stefan Sagmeister, "Stefan Sagmeister: The Power of Time Off" (video file), TEDGlobal 2009, July 2009, http://www.ted.com/talks/stefan_sagmeister_the_power_of_time_off?language=en (accessed May 12, 2015).

2. Ibid.

3. Society for Human Resource Management (SHRM), *2009 Employee Benefits: Examining Employee Benefits in a Fiscally Challenging Economy* (Alexandria, VA: SHRM, 2009).

4. Society for Human Resource Management (SHRM), *2014 Employee Benefits: An Overview of Employee Benefit Offerings in the US* (Alexandria, VA: SHRM, 2014).

5. Tamson Pietsch, "What's Happened to Sabbatical Leave for Academics?" *The Guardian,* October 5, 2011.

6. Walter Crosby Eells and Ernest V. Hollis, *Sabbatical Leave in American Higher Education: Origin, Early History, and Current Practices,* Bulletin 17, OE-53016 (Washington, DC: US Department of Health, Education, and Welfare, Office of Education, 1962).

7. Grid Business, "How the Lucky Few with Paid Sabbaticals Are Using Their Time," *Chicago Sun-Times,* April 8, 2013.

8. Ibid.

9. Kathryn Tyler, "Sabbaticals Pay Off," *HR Magazine,* December 1, 2011, http://www.shrm.org/publications/hrmagazine/editorialcontent/2011/1211/pages/1211tyler.aspx (accessed April 29, 2015).

10. YourSabbatical.com, "Workplaces for Sabbaticals," http://yoursabbatical.com/learn/workplaces-for-sabbaticals (accessed April 28, 2015).

11. Build Network staff, "Why Paid Sabbaticals Are Good for Employees and Employers," Inc. 5000, December 25, 2013, http://www.inc.com/the-build-network/why-paid-sabbaticals-are-good-for-employees-and-employers.html (accessed April 29, 2015).

12. Ibid.

13. Morningstar, "Morningstar Benefits for US Employees," http://corporate1.morningstar.com/us/Careers/Benefits/ (accessed April 29, 2015).

14. Terri Lee Ryan, "Morningstar: The Company That Works!" ChicagoNow, March 18, 2011, http://www.chicagonow.com/get-employed/2011/03/morningstar-the-company-that-works/ (accessed April 29, 2015).

15. Oranit B. Davidson, Dov Eden, Mina Westman, Yochi Cohen-Charash, Leslie B. Hammer, Avraham N. Kluger, Moshe Krausz, Christina Maslach, Michael O'Driscoll, Pamela L. Perrewé, James Campbell Quick, Zehava Rosenblatt, and Paul E. Spector, "Sabbatical Leave: Who Gains and How Much?" *Journal of Applied Psychology* 95, no. 5 (2010): 953.

16. Alexandra Levit, "Should Companies Offer Sabbaticals?" *Fortune,* January 3, 2011.

17. Davidson et al., "Sabbatical Leave," 953.

18. Levit, "Should Companies Offer Sabbaticals?"

19. Deborah Linnell and Tim Wolfred, *Creative Disruption: Sabbaticals for Capacity Building and Leadership Development in the Non-profit Sector* (Boston: Third Sector New England and CompassPoint, 2010).

20. Ibid., 24.
21. Minda Zetlin, "Five Surprisingly Good Reason to Pay — Yes, Pay! — Employees to Go on Vacation," *Inc.*, April 3, 2015, http://www.inc.com/minda-zetlin/5-surprisingly-good-reasons-to-pay-yes-pay-employees-to-go-on-vacation.html (accessed April 29, 2015).
22. Sue Shellengarger, "Companies Deal with Employees Who Refuse to Take Time Off by Requiring Vacations, Paying Them to Go," *Wall Street Journal*, August 12, 2014.
23. Rachel Feintzeig, "Cure for Office Burnout: Mini Sabbaticals," *Wall Street Journal*, October 28, 2014.
24. Will Oremus, (2014). "You Deserve a Pre-cation: The Smartest Job Perk You've Never Heard Of," *Slate*, September 30, 2014, http://www.slate.com/articles/business/building_a_better_workplace/2014/09/precation_perks_companies_offer_employees_vacation_before_they_start.html (accessed April 20, 3015).
25. Ibid.
26. Ibid.
27. Emily McManus, "Why TED Takes Two Weeks Off Every Summer," TED Blog, July 17, 2014, http://blog.ted.com/why-ted-takes-two-weeks-off-every-summer/ (accessed April 20, 2015).

12. Fire the Managers

1. Michael Abrash, "Valve: How I Got Here, What It's Like, and What I'm Doing," Ramblings in Valve Time, April 13, 2012, http://blogs.valvesoftware.com/abrash/valve-how-i-got-here-what-its-like-and-what-im-doing-2/ (accessed May 12, 2015).
2. Valve, *Handbook for Employees* (Kirkland, WA: Valve Press, 2012).
3. Leerom Segal, Aaron Goldstein, Jay Goldman, and Rahaf Harfoush, *The Decoded Company: Know Your Talent Better Than You Know Your Customers* (New York: Portfolio, 2014).
4. Samuel Walreich, "A Billion-Dollar Company with No Boss Exists," *Inc.*, March 4, 2013, http://www.inc.com/samuel-wagreich/the-4-billion-company-with-no-bosses.html (accessed May 12, 2015).
5. Claire Suddath, "Why There Are No Bosses at Valve," *Bloomberg BusinessWeek*, April 27, 2012, http://www.bloomberg.com/bw/articles/2012-04-27/why-there-are-no-bosses-at-valve (accessed May 15, 2015).
6. Valve, *Handbook for Employees*, 4.
7. Walreich, "A Billion-Dollar Company with No Boss Exists."

8. Jacob Morgan, *The Future of Work: Attract New Talent, Build Better Leaders, and Create a Competitive Organization* (Hoboken, NJ: Wiley, 2014), 47–48.

9. Valve, *Handbook for Employees*, 44.

10. Ibid., 6.

11. Daniel H. Pink, *Drive: The Surprising Truth About What Motivates Us* (New York: Riverhead, 2009).

12. Edward L. Deci and Richard M. Ryan, "Facilitating Optimal Motivation and Psychological Well-being Across Life's Domains," *Canadian Psychology/Psychologie canadienne* 49, no. 1 (2008): 14.

13. Richard M. Locke and Monica Romis, "Improving Work Conditions in a Global Supply Chain," *MIT Sloan Management Review* (January 2007).

14. Kamal Birdi, Chris Clegg, Malcolm Patterson, Andrew Robinson, Chris B. Stride, Toby D. Wall, and Stephen J. Wood, "The Impact of Human Resource and Operational Management Practices on Company Productivity: A Longitudinal Study," *Personnel Psychology* 61, no. 3 (2008): 467–501.

15. Muammer Ozer, "A Moderated Mediation Model of the Relationship Between Organizational Citizenship Behaviors and Job Performance," *Journal of Applied Psychology* 96, no. 6 (2011): 1328–36.

16. Deci and Ryan, "Facilitating Optimal Motivation," 15–16.

17. Valery Chirkov, Richard M. Ryan, Youngmee Kim, and Ulas Kaplan, "Differentiating Autonomy from Individualism and Independence: A Self-determination Theory Perspective on Internalization of Cultural Orientations and Well-being," *Journal of Personality and Social Psychology* 84, no. 1 (2003): 97–110; Joseph Devine, Laura Camfield, and Ian Gough, "Autonomy or Dependence — or Both? Perspectives from Bangladesh," *Journal of Happiness Studies* 9, no. 1 (2008): 105–38.

18. Herb Kelleher, "A Culture of Commitment," *Leader to Leader* 4 (1997): 20–24.

19. First Round Review, (2014, July 15). "Can Holacracy Work? How Medium Functions Without Managers," *Fast Company,* July 15, 2014, http://www .fastcompany.com/3032994/can-holacracy-work-how-medium-functions -without-managers (accessed May 13, 2015).

20. Gary Hamel, "First, Let's Fire All the Managers," *Harvard Business Review* 89, no. 12 (2011): 48–60.

21. Ibid., 52.

22. Ibid.

23. Ibid., 54.

24. Ibid.

25. Ibid., 52.

26. John Paul Titlow, "210 Zappos Employees Respond to Holacracy Ultimatum: We're Out," *Fast Company*, May 8, 2015, http://www.fastcompany.com/3046121/fast-feed/210-zappos-employees-respond-to-holacracy-ultimatum-were-out (accessed May 14, 2015).

27. Charles Fishman, "How Team Work Took Flight," *Fast Company*, 1999, http://www.fastcompany.com/38322/how-teamwork-took-flight (accessed May 14, 2015).

28. Ibid.

29. Ibid.

30. Darren Dahl, "Kim Jordon on Why Employee-Owned New Belgium Brewing Isn't Worried About a Craft Beer Bubble," *Forbes*, May 5, 2015.

31. Leigh Buchanan, "It's All About Ownership," *Inc.*, April 18, 2013, http://www.inc.com/audacious-companies/leigh-buchanan/new-belgium-brewing.html (accessed May 15, 2015).

32. Michelle Goodman, "How to Build an Employee-Owned Business," *Entrepreneur*, February 23, 2015, http://www.entrepreneur.com/article/241522 (accessed May 15, 2015).

33. Katie Wallace, "The Power of Employee Ownership: New Belgium," *Conscious Company Magazine*, Winter 2015, http://www.consciouscompanymagazine.com/blogs/press/16248541-the-power-of-employee-ownership-new-belgium (accessed May 15, 2015).

34. Dahl, "Kim Jordon on Why Employee-Owned New Belgium Brewing."

13. Celebrate Departures

1. Daniel Cohen and Sean Brown, "Global Leaders Summit 2014: Sean Brown" (video file), December 3, 2014, https://www.youtube.com/watch?v=kHU2kt7mQdA (accessed April 3, 2015).

2. McKinsey & Company, "Alumni — A Community for Life," http://www.mckinsey.com/careers/our_people_and_values/alumni-a_community_for_life (accessed April 2, 2015).

3. Andrew Hill, "Inside McKinsey," *Financial Times*, November 25, 2011.

4. Duff McDonald, "The Answer Men," *New York*, July 27, 2009.

5. Hill, "Inside McKinsey."

6. Duff McDonald, *The Firm: The Story of McKinsey and Its Secret Influence on American Business* (New York: Simon & Schuster, 2014).

7. Cohen and Brown, "Global Leaders Summit 2014: Sean Brown."

8. Ibid.

9. Brian Uzzi, personal communication with the author, March 23, 2015.

10. Brian Uzzi, "The Sources and Consequences of Embeddedness for the Economic Performance of Organizations: The Network Effect," *American Sociological Review* 61, no. 4 (1996): 674–98.

11. Uzzi, personal communication with the author, March 23, 2015.

12. Ibid.

13. Cohen and Brown, "Global Leaders Summit 2014: Sean Brown."

14. Ibid.

15. Joe Laufer, "Corporate Alumni Programmes: What Universities Can Learn from the Business Experience," November 5, 2009, http://www.slideshare .net/joeinholland/what-universities-can-learn-from-corporate-alumni -programs (accessed April 23, 2015).

16. Reid Hoffman, Ben Casnocha, and Chris Yeh, *The Alliance: Managing Talent in the Networked Age* (Boston: Harvard Business Review Press, 2014).

17. Ibid., 140.

18. Ibid., 144.

19. Microsoft Alumni Network, "About Us," https://www.microsoftalumni.com /about-us (accessed April 21, 2015).

20. Todd Bishop, "Microsoft Alumni Groups Combine, Aim to Expand, Led by Former Exec Jeff Raikes," *GeekWire*, June 26, 2014, http://www.geekwire.com /2014/microsoft-alumni-groups-combine-aim-expand-led-former-exec -jeff-raikes/ (accessed April 21, 2015).

21. Emily Glazer, "Leave the Company, but Stay in Touch," *Wall Street Journal*, December 20, 2012.

22. P&G Alumni Network, "About," http://www.pgalums.com (accessed April 21, 2015).

23. Big Four Firms Network, "Accenture Alumni Network Is a Win-Win Proposition," http://www.big4.com/news/accenture-alumni-network-is-a-win-win -proposition/ (accessed April 20, 2015).

24. Jennifer Salopek, "Employee Referrals Remain a Recruiter's Best Friend," *Workforce*, December 6, 2010, http://www.workforce.com/articles/employee -referrals-remain-a-recruiters-best-friend (accessed April 20, 2015).

25. Chevron, "Join Chevron Alumni and Bridges for Contract Positions," http: //alumni.chevron.com (accessed April 20, 2015).

26. L. M. Sixel, "Chevron Woos Ex-employees Back as Contractors," *Houston Chronicle*, February 10, 2010.

Afterword: Reinventing the Management Engine

1. Yunus A. Cengel and Michael A. Boles, *Thermodynamics: An Engineering Approach*, 4th ed. (New York: McGraw-Hill, 2015), 496.

2. Steve Crabtree, "Worldwide, 13% of Employees Are Engaged at Work," Gallup, October 8, 2013, http://www.gallup.com/poll/165269/worldwide-employ ees-engaged-at-work.aspx (accessed May 26, 2015).

3. Amy Adkins, "Majority of US Employees Not Engaged Despite Gains in 2014," Gallup, January 28, 2015, http://www.gallup.com/poll/181289/majority -employees-not-engaged-despite-gains-2014.aspx (accessed May 26, 2015).

4. Dane Atkinson, Personal communication with the author, February 26, 2015.

Index

Abrash, Michael, 177
Accenture, 203–4
Adams, John Stacey, 79, 83
Adobe Systems, 8, 102–8, 113, 116,
    166
Advertising Age, 149
Akerlof, George, 73–74
Almaden Lab, 98–99
alumni networks. *See* departures,
    celebrating
Amabile, Teresa, 146
Amazon, 8, 62, 67–68, 79
American Bar Association (ABA),
    90
American Psychological Association,
    131
Amir, On, 95, 96
amygdala, 50
Ariely, Dan, 66
Arkes, Hal, 63
arm's-length vs. close-knit ties,
    197–98, 201, 204, 205
Atkinson, Dane, 71–72, 74–76, 81, 83,
    84, 144, 208, 209
Atlassian, 16–17, 174
Atos SE, 13–14, 17, 18, 20, 22
Autodesk, 166
Automattic, 125–28, 131
autonomy. *See* managers, companies
    without

Baard, Paul, 181
Bamberger, Peter, 78, 81, 82, 85
Becker, William, 24
Belogolovsky, Elena, 78, 81, 82, 85
Benchley, Robert, 72–73
benefits, employment, 36–38, 42.
    See also health insurance;
    vacation policies
Bethlehem Iron Company, 1–2, 3, 11,
    207
Bezos, Jeff, 67–68
Birdi, Kamal, 182
Birkinshaw, Julian, 6
Bloomberg, Michael, 151
BlueKiwi, 15
Blumer, Catherine, 63
Bock, Laszlo, 129
Boswell, Wendy, 24
Bower, Marvin, 193–94
brain, 50, 52
Brand, Jay, 157, 160
Branson, Sir Richard, 47–48, 49, 53, 57
Brehm, Jack, 65–66
Breton, Thierry, 13–14, 17, 18, 22
Brin, Sergey, 129
Broadway, 141–43, 144
Brown, Greg, 115
Brown, Sean, 193, 195
Brown, Steven, 33–34
Brummel, Lisa, 113, 114

Buffer, 76–77, 78, 81, 82, 84
Buser, Cimarron, 87
Buser, Colette, 87
Businessweek (magazine), 4
Butts, Marcus, 24, 25

California, 83, 91, 99
CannonDesign, 158
Card, David, 83, 84
Cardello, Armand, 17
Carman, Zac, 48–49, 57
Carnegie Steel Company, 1
Center for Organizational
        Effectiveness (American
        Psychological Association), 131
check-in process, 105–7
Chevron, 204–5
"Chevron Bridges" program, 204–5
Chiat, Jay, 148–50, 152, 158, 160, 161
Chiat/Day, 148–50, 152, 158–61
Chicago Tribune, 53
Christensen, Clay, 139–40
Cicotello, Sam, 173
Cisco Systems, 151
City University of Hong Kong, 182
Claremont Graduate University, 50
Claremont's Center for
        Neuroeconomics Studies, 50
Clegg, Chris, 154
close-knit vs. arm's-length ties,
        197–98, 201, 204, 205
cognitive dissonance, 65–66
Cohen, June, 174, 175
Colleague Letter of Understanding
        (CLOU), 185–86
Comnet, 27
confirmation bias, 8
Connect + Develop, 100–101
Connects (meetings), 114

consulting firms
    open vs. closed offices at, 159–61
    organizational charts of, 132–36,
        139
    See also Accenture; Eden
        McCallum; McKinsey &
        Company
ConsumerAffairs, 48–49, 56
Cornell University, 78, 154
Corredoira, Rafael, 93, 99
Craig, David, 158
Culbertson, Satoris, 111–12
customer loyalty, 32–33, 38, 42

Daimler, 23–24
Danish Work Environment Cohort
        Study, 156
Dartmouth College, 4
Davis, Matthew, 154
Day, Guy, 148
Deci, Edward, 180–81, 183
de Dear, Richard, 153
departures, celebrating, 10, 192–205
    embeddedness/networks in,
        196–99
    growth/variety of alumni networks
        in, 199–205
    at McKinsey & Company, 192–96,
        198–99, 202, 203, 205
Diana, Jeff, 174
DiDonato, Tom, 114
Directions, 31
Discretionary Time Off (DTO), 53,
        54
disruptive innovation, 139–40
Driscoll, Mark, 88–89
Drucker, Peter, 121, 138
Duke University, 66
Dweck, Carol, 110

Economic Times, 103, 105
Eden, Liann, 133, 134, 135, 140, 143
Eden McCallum, 132–36, 139–40, 143,
    144, 147
el Mejor Trato (eMT), 17
email, limiting, 7, 13–25
    Atlassian president on use of email,
        16–17
    at Atos SE, 13–16, 17, 18, 20, 22
    at Daimler, 23–24
    at el Mejor Trato (eMT), 17
    Evernote CEO on email volume,
        16
    in France, 23
    in Germany, 23–24
    at Learning as Leadership, 19, 20
    policy of moderation for, 20
    research on, 17–21, 24–25
    social networks for, 15, 16
    at Volkswagen, 22–23
    to workday hours, 22–25
    working memory and, 21–22
embeddedness, 196–99
employees first, customers second, 7,
    26–43
    at HCL Technologies (HCLT),
        26–32
    research on, 32–35
    at Starbucks, 39–43
    at Union Square Hospitality Group,
        37–39
    at Wegmans Food Markets, 35–37,
        39
engagement, 208
equity theory, 79–80, 82, 83
Ernst & Young, 150–51
Evans, Gary, 154, 156
Evernote, 16
Expedia, Inc., 115–16

Facebook, 47, 151
feedback
    discussions replacing annual
        reviews, 114
    360-degree system of, 30–31
    at Union Square Café, 38
Festinger, Leon, 65
Financieele Dagblad, 140
Fleming, Lee, 92, 93, 99
Floersch, Rich, 165
"Fool's Errand, the," 172–73
forced ranking systems, 109, 115
Fordham University, 181
Fortune (magazine), 5, 37, 62, 119
42Floors, 173–74
France, 23–24
Freedman, Jason, 173, 174
Frenken, Koen, 99
FullContact software company,
    171–72

gainsharing, 120
Gallup Organization, 64, 68, 208
garment industry, research study on
        networks in, 196–98
Gascoigne, Joel, 76–77, 83, 84–85
Gehry, Frank, 151
General Electric, 79, 187–89
German Labor Ministry, 23
Germany, 23–24
Gerson Lehrman Group, Inc. (GLG),
    159–61
Google, 99, 128–30, 131
Gore, Bill, 145
Graham, Tami, 165–66
Griffin, Jack, 54
groupthink, 5
Groysberg, Boris, 122, 123, 124,
    129

Half-Life game series, 177
Hamel, Gary, 10
Hammarplast, 39–40
Harrington, Mike, 177, 178
Harvard Business Review, 114, 128, 138
Harvard Business School, 92, 121, 146, 194
Harvard University, 32, 35, 164
Hastings, Reed, 6, 45–46, 47, 49, 56–57
Haworth, 157
Hawthorne Works study, 108
HCL Technologies (HCLT), 26–35
health insurance, 36–37, 40, 42
Heiferman, Scott, 166
Helm, Jelly, 98
Henderson, Robert, 187–88, 189
Henshaw, George Holt, 137
Heskett, James, 32, 35
Hewlett-Packard, 99
hiring as a team, 9, 117–31
    at Automattic with trial process, 125–28, 131
    at Google, 128–30, 131
    job performance and, 121–25
    at Steelscape, 130–31
    at Whole Foods Market, 117–20, 125, 131
Hoffman, Reid, 199–201
Hsieh, Tony, 59–62, 67, 186, 187
Huet-Vaughn, Emiliano, 79, 82, 85
Hughes, Shayne, 19, 20
human relations movement, 108

IBM, 98–99
IDEO, 145–47
India, 27, 31, 102–3
industrial revolution, 3

information asymmetry, 73–74
INSEAD, 92, 133, 141
Institute for Women's Policy Research, 82
Institutional Investor, 123
"Integral Fellows" program, 202
Intel, 99, 165, 166
internal combustion engine analogy, 206–10
internal service quality, 33, 35
International Ladies' Garment Workers' Union (ILGWU), 196–97
investment game, 50–52

Janus, Irving, 5
Japan, 4
jewelry workers, research on autonomy with, 182–83
Jimmy John's Gourmet Sandwiches, 87–88
Johnson, Dana, 154, 156
Jones, Thomas, 32
Jordon, Kim, 189, 191

Kahn, Joe, 87
Kansas State University, 111
Kelleher, Herb, 183
Kelley, David, 145–46
Kennedy, David, 97
Kim, Jungsoo, 153
knowledge work, 5, 7, 138, 181, 208, 209
Kushlev, Kostadin, 21, 22

Lafley, A.G., 100, 101, 202
Lam, Son, 33–34
Lawler, Edward, 81
Leach, Desmond, 154

Leadership Conference (Starbucks), 42
"League of Legends" video game, 69
Lear Corporation, 114, 116
Learning as Leadership, 19
Lebesch, Jeff, 189, 190, 191
Ledbetter, Lilly, 81–82
Lee, Young, 157, 160
LEED-certification assessments, 153
Libin, Phil, 16
lift-outs, 123, 124, 125
Lilly Ledbetter Fair Pay Act of 2009, 82
Lin, Alfred, 60
LinkedIn, 199–201
LinkExchange, 60
Linnell, Deborah, 169–71
LINX camps, 87
Lobel, Orly, 95, 96
Locke, Richard, 181
Loma Linda University, 50
London Business School, 6
Lorang, Bart, 171–72
Los Angeles Times, 53–54
Loveman, Gary, 32

Mackey, John, 77–78, 118–20
managers, companies without, 10, 176–91
    General Electric (Durham, North Carolina), 187–89
    Medium software company, 184
    Morning Star Company, 184–86, 191
    New Belgium Brewing
        experimenting with autonomy for employees, 189–91
    the origins of autonomy for, 180–84
    trend in software/technology world, 184

Valve Software, 176–79, 181, 183, 188, 191
Zappos, 186–87
Mansueto, Joe, 166
manual vs. mental labor, 5. *See also* knowledge work
manufacturers, autonomy and, 182
Mark, Gloria, 17–19, 20
Marshall School of Business (University of Southern California), 81
Mars Hill megachurch, 88–89
Martin, Roger, 138–39
Marx, Matt, 92–93
Mayo, Elton, 108
McCallum, Daniel, 136–37, 145
McCallum, Dena, 133, 134
McCord, Patty, 47
McDonald's, 164–65, 166
McGovern, Brendan, 166
McKinsey, James O., 193
McKinsey & Company, 133, 192–96, 198–99, 202, 203
Mechanical Turk platform (MTurk), 79
Medium software company, 184
MeetUp, 166
Menlo Innovations, 166
mental vs. manual labor, 5. *See also* knowledge work
Meyer, Danny, 37–38, 43
Michigan, 92–93
Michigan Antitrust Reform Act (MARA), 92–93
Microsoft, 8, 60, 99, 113–14, 116, 201–2, 203, 205
Microsoft Alumni Foundation, 201
Microsoft Alumni Network, 201, 202
Middlebury College, 79

misguided hero syndrome, 172, 173
MIT (Massachusetts Institute of
    Technology), 195
Morningstar, 166–67
Morning Star Company, 184–86, 191
Morris, Donna, 102–7, 113
Motley Fool, 172–73
Motorola, 8, 114–15, 116
Mullenweg, Matt, 125–28
Musyj, David, 55–56, 57

Nayar, Vineet, 26–35, 43
Netemeyer, Richard, 34–35
Netflix, 6, 44–49, 53, 56
networks, 141–47
    arm's length vs. close-knit ties,
        197–98, 201, 204, 205
    departures, celebrating, 10, 192–205
    embeddedness, 196–99
    growth/variety of alumni networks,
        199–205
    at McKinsey & Company, 192–96,
        198–99, 202, 203, 205
neuroeconomics, 50
New Belgium Brewing, 189–91
Newell, Gabe, 177, 178
New York and Erie Railway, 137
New York Times, 87, 109
Nike, 181–82
noncompete clauses/agreements, 8,
    86–101
    banned in California, 91, 99
    current use of, 90, 101
    history of rejecting, 89–90
    at Jimmy John's Gourmet
        Sandwiches, 87–88
    at LINX camps, 87
    at Mars Hill megachurch, 88–89
    in Michigan, 92–93

non-noncompete environments vs.,
    97–101
research on, 92–96, 99
Silicon Valley vs. Route 128, 91–92
Northwestern University, 141

Obama, Barack, 82
offices. See open vs. closed offices
"100 Best Companies to Work For"
    list, 37, 62, 119
Onward (Schultz), 41
open vs. closed offices, 9, 148–60
    at Chiat/Day, 148–50, 152, 159, 160,
        161
    at Cisco Systems, 151
    control as issue in, 157–61
    at Ernst & Young, 150–51
    at Facebook, 151
    noise and, 153–54, 156, 157–61
    in office of New York City mayor,
        151
    percentage of open offices
        currently, 151
    research on, 151–58
    sick days and, 156–57
    at Sprint, 151
organizational charts/hierarchy, 9, 35,
    132–47
    Broadway and, 141–44
    at Chiat/Day, 157
    CLOU (Colleague Letter of
        Understanding) as, 185–86
    at Eden McCallum consulting firm,
        132–36, 139–40, 143, 144, 147
    employees first, customers second
        and, 29, 31, 34
    at IDEO, 145–47
    knowledge work and, 138–39
    origins of, 136–38

organizational charts/hierarchy, (*cont.*)
  at SumAll, 144, 145, 147
  at W. L. Gore, 145, 147
Organization Man, The (Whyte), 5
Oxford University, 194
oxytocin, 50, 52
Ozer, Muammer, 182

P&G Alumni Foundation, 203
Page, Larry, 129, 130
paid-paid vacations, 171–72
parental leaves, 46
Parker, Dorothy, 72–73
payroll. *See* salary transparency
Pay to Quit program, 67–68
Pejtersen, Jan, 156
Penn State Law Review, 82
performance
  autonomy and, 181, 182, 183
  open vs. closed offices and, 152
  sabbaticals and, 173
  salary transparency and, 78–80
  teams and, 121–22
  Wall Street and, 121–24
  See also performance appraisals
performance appraisals, 8–9, 102–16
  at Adobe Systems, 102–8, 113, 116
  for company without managers, 179
  at Expedia, Inc., 115–16
  at General Electric, 108–9
  history of, 108
  at Lear Corporation, 114, 116
  at Microsoft, 113–14, 116
  at Motorola, 114–15, 116
  research on, 110–12
  Sutton on, 109–10
  See also performance
Performance Rating Act of 1950, 108
Perstorp AB, 39

Phillips Exeter Academy, 1
piece-rate system, 2
post-decision dissonance, 65–66, 68
Post-Occupancy Evaluation (POE)
    database, 153
pre-cations, 173–74, 175
Predictably Irrational (Ariely), 66
Principles of Scientific Management
    (Taylor), 4
Proctor & Gamble, 99–101, 202–3
Proctor & Gamble Alumni Network,
    202–3
productivity
  autonomy and, 182, 191
  email and, 18–22, 25
  employee satisfaction and, 33
  hiring as a team and, 131
  Mayo on, 108
  noncompete clauses/agreements
    and, 95, 97
  open offices and, 151, 153, 154, 156,
    157
  quitting bonuses and, 68
  salary transparency and, 73
  trust and, 52
profitability
  customer loyalty and, 32–33
  effect of limiting email on, 18
  employees first, customers second
    and, 35
  engagement and, 208

Q scores, 142, 144, 147
Queue Dodge program, 69
Quick, James Campbell, 168, 169
QuikTrip, 167
quitting bonuses, 8, 58–70
  at Amazon, 67–68
  reasons for, 62–67

at Riot Games, 69
at Zappos, 58–62, 64–69

Ramachandran, Gowri, 82
rank-and-yank system. *See* forced
    ranking systems
*Reference Guide on Our Freedom and
    Responsibility Culture* (Netflix
    slide deck), 46–49
Reichheld, Fred, 32
remote associates task, 95
Rennella, Cristian, 17
reverse accountability, 29–30, 31
"right to know" law (in California), 83
Riot Games, 69
Rosenkopf, Lori, 93, 99
Rotman School of Management, 138
Route 128 (in Boston), 91–92
Rufer, Chris, 185, 186
Ryan, Richard, 180–81, 183

sabbaticals, 9–10, 162–75
    in academic world, 164, 168
    at Atlassian, 174
    benefits of, 167–69
    increasing number of, in corporate
        America, 163–64
    at Intel, 165, 166
    as leadership development, 169–71
    at McDonald's, 164–65, 166
    mini-, 171–75
    at Morningstar, 166–67
    at Motley Fool, 172–73
    at QuikTrip, 167
    research on, 168–71
    Sagmeister on, 162–63, 174, 175
    at technology companies, 165–66
Sacramento Bee, 83
Saferway, 118

Sagmeister, Stefan, 162–63, 174–75
Saint-Amand, Alexander, 159, 160, 161
salary transparency, 8, 71–85
    Atkinson and, 71–72, 74–76, 81, 83,
        84, 208
    at Buffer, 76–77, 78, 81, 82, 84
    equity theory and, 79–80, 82, 83
    information asymmetry and, 73–74
    legal reasons for, 81–82
    research on, 78–80, 81, 83–84, 85
    at SumAll, 74–76, 78, 82, 84, 85
    at *Vanity Fair* (magazine), 72–73
    at Whole Foods Market, 77–78, 84
Sandberg, Sheryl, 47
Sasser, W. Earl, 32
Saxenian, AnnaLee, 92
Schlesinger, Leonard, 32
Schultz, Howard, 39–43
scientific management, 2–6, 193
Securities and Exchange Commission,
    120
self-determination theory, 180
Sequoia Capital, 62
service-profit chain, 31, 33, 35, 37, 42
Shake Shack, 38
Sherwood, Robert, 72–73
Silicon Valley, 47, 91, 92, 99, 165–66
Simons, Jay, 16–17
Singh, Jasjit, 92–93
Sloan School of Management (MIT),
    195, 198
smart service desk, 29
Society for Human Resource
    Management, 163
Southwest Airlines, 183
Southwestern Law School, 82
Spence, Michael, 73–74
Spiro, Jarrett, 141–43
Sprint, 151

stack ranking systems, 103–4, 113. *See also* forced ranking systems
Stanford University, 98, 109, 110
Starbucks, 39–43
Steam, 177
Steelscape, 130–31
stepping stones, 186
Stiglitz, Joseph E., 73–74
stock options, 120
SumAll
    organizational charts at, 144, 145, 147
    salary transparency at, 8, 74–76, 78, 82, 84, 85, 208
sunk costs, 8, 63–64, 67
Sutton, Bob, 109–10
Swinmurn, Nick, 59–60
Symes, Connie, 115, 116
System magazine, 4
Syzdek, D'Renda, 205

Taylor, Frederick Winslow, 1–4, 5, 11, 108, 130, 193, 207, 209
Tazzia, Ed, 202
TBWA/Chiat Day. *See* Chiat/Day
teams/teamwork
    managers/management and, 178–79, 181–82, 184, 187–89
    organizational charts and, 134–35, 141–47
    performance appraisals and, 113–14
    team-building at Starbucks, 42
    See also hiring as a team
TEDGlobal conference, 162–63, 174–75
Tel Aviv University, 78
training
    at Eden McCallum consulting firm, 135

employees first, customers second and, 36, 40
    at McKinsey & Company, 193
    at New Belgium Brewing, 190
    performance appraisals and, 107
    quitting bonuses and, 59
    sunk costs and, 64
transparency, building, 29, 30–31
travel/expenses policies, 46–47
trials hiring process, 125–28
Tribune Publishing, 53–55, 56
trust, 49–57, 76
Tuck School of Business (Dartmouth College), 4

Union Square Café, 38
Union Square Hospitality Group, 37–39
University of Athens, 178
University of British Columbia, 20
University of Calgary, 152
University of California at Berkeley, 79, 83, 153
University of California at Irvine, 17
University of Houston, 33
University of Leeds, 154
University of Maryland, 93
University of Rochester, 180
University of San Diego, 95
University of Sheffield, 182
University of Southern California, 81
University of Sydney, 153, 164
University of Texas at Arlington, 168
University of Virginia, 34
US Army, 17
Uzzi, Brian, 141–43, 196–99, 205

vacation policies, 7, 44–57
    at ConsumerAffairs, 48–49, 56
    email, 23–24
    at Netflix, 44–49, 53, 56
    at Tribune Publishing, 53–55
    trust and, 49–57
    at Virgin Group, 47–48, 56
    at Windsor Regional Hospital,
        55–56
    See also pre-cations
value, service-profit chain and, 33
values
    at Buffer, 76
    at Starbucks, 42
    at Zappos, 59, 61
value zones, 28, 29
Valve Software, 176–79, 181, 183, 188,
    191
Vanity Fair (magazine), 72–73, 113
Varoufakis, Yanis, 178
Venture Frogs, 60
Virgin Group, 47–48, 56
virtuous cycle of enlightened
        hospitality, 37, 38
Voida, Stephen, 17–18
Volkswagen (company), 22–23

Wallace, Katie, 190
Wall Street, 121–24

Wegman, Danny, 35–36
Wegman, John, 35
Wegman, Walter, 35
Wegmans Food Markets, 35–37, 39
Welch, Jack, 108–9, 113
Western Electric Company, 108
Wharton School, 93
When Prophecy Fails (Festinger), 65
Whole Foods Market, 8, 77–78, 84,
        117–18, 125
Whyte, William, 5
Wieden, Dan, 97
Wieden+Kennedy (W+K), 97–98
Wilkinson, Clive, 160, 161
Windsor Regional Hospital, 55–56
Wired (magazine), 149
WK12 (W+K advertising school),
        97–98
W. L. Gore, 145, 147
Wolfred, Tim, 169–71
WordPress, 125, 128

Yahoo!, 99
Yonsei University, 157

Zak, Paul, 50–52, 56
Zappos, 8, 58–62, 64–69, 186–87
Zobele, 100
Zuckerberg, Mark, 151

About the Author

David Burkus is a best-selling author, an award-winning podcaster, and a management professor. In 2015, he was named one of the emerging thought leaders most likely to shape the future of business by Thinkers50, the world's premier ranking of management thinkers.

David is a regular contributor to *Harvard Business Review* and *Forbes*. His work has been featured in *Fast Company, Inc.,* the *Financial Times, Bloomberg Businessweek,* and *CBS This Morning.* His previous book, *The Myths of Creativity: The Truth About How Innovative Companies and People Generate Great Ideas,* replaced the misconceptions that companies have about creativity with evidence-based strategies for innovation.

David's views on leadership, innovation, and strategy have earned him invitations to speak to leaders from a variety of organizations. He has delivered keynote speeches and workshops for Fortune 500 companies such as Microsoft, Google, and Stryker, appeared at in-demand conferences such as SXSW and TEDx events, and spoken before governmental leaders and military leaders at the US Naval Academy and Naval Postgraduate School. He's also the host of the award-winning podcast *Radio Free Leader.*

When he's not speaking or writing, David is in the classroom. He is associate professor of management at Oral Roberts University, where he teaches courses on organizational behavior, creativity and innovation, and strategic leadership. David was recently named one of the "Top 40 Under 40 Professors Who Inspire." He serves on the advisory board of Fuse Corps, a nonprofit dedicated to making transformative and replicable change in local government.

David lives in Tulsa with his wife and their two boys.